AF820600

This Book

This book was written to explain how to use Conitec's 3D Gamestudio.
For more information visit **http://www.create3dgames.com**

Copyright

Trademarks

Disclaimer

Table of Contents

Chapter 3 - Textures con't ----

Chapter 4 - Primitives ------ 60

Chapter 5 - Entities ------ 76

Chapter 1 - **Introduction**

Before you Start

Download - 3dGamestudio software from **Conitec 3dGamestudio**
http://www.3dgamestudio.com

Download - **lite-C software**. http://www.3dgamestudio.com/

Download - **Paint.net**. Paint.net is a free image and photo editing software. There is an active online community involved with Paint.net. http://www.getpaint.net

3D Gamestudio Software

Select your Edition

"You have the choice of four upwards compatible 2D/3D application development systems. All include lite-C and the same powerful A8 engine and physics engine. They only differ in features:

Gamestudio Free is for classical game development. It comes with all tools for creating great casual 2D and 3D games.
Gamestudio Extra has similar features as the free edition, but precompiles your script - so games will start faster, and people can't see or modify your code.
Gamestudio Commercial can create network and online games, and supports high-end graphical effects such as postprocessing shaders, decals and beams.
Gamestudio Pro is for large scale games and MMOG projects. (Massively Multiplayer Online Game) It contains special technologies for ultra-fast rendering, and special features for commercial distribution.
Educational Edition
All editions are 100% up- and downwards compatible. Try before buying? Download the free version, open the tutorial, and start creating games!"
Conitec - 2011 - Information from Conitec website.

The MED is the Model Editor, the SED is the Script Editor. This book explains the WED Editor.

Gamestudio World Editor

The **World Editor**, WED is Gamestudio's main editor. WED is where the editor creates the Virtual World or level. Users can create games by designing their own environments and creating and importing models. The software allows users to add textures, create scripts, designs, give models attributes and actions, add sound, add properties such as fluidity and create and add backgrounds. This book focuses on the WED editor.

The World Editor- WED is the location where users merge all the components.

Users of Gamestudio can **import file formats** from other computer games such as Quake. Pre-constructed **levels** (MAP files), **textures** (WAD files) and **3D models** (MDL or 3D files) can be imported into Gamestudio.

What's in This Book

This book is for new users of Conitec's Gamestudio software. The book is written as a visual guide for understanding how Gamestudio's WED World Level Editor works. The book is filled with examples and screen shots to "show" the reader how to use Conitec's 3dGamestudio software. Not every menu item will be covered. This book is for a new user who wants to master the basics right away and get started as quickly as possible. A book this size cannot possibly cover every aspect of the WED. The book does contain information for building a level and a basic game. Several tips and hints will speed up the learning process for the novice and may fill in some missing information for other users of the gamestudio software. This is a Step-by-Step Instruction book that introduces the basics and shows the reader how to use the WED level editor.

The book will start with the absolute basics of adding a cube, hollowing it and starting the process of creating a room. Texturing is explained and how to use Paint.net, a free software program, to create custom textures. Primitives are explained. Instructions are included on how to use Gamestudio's basic primitives to create and texture levels. The models (players) used in the book are models that have been downloaded from Gamestudio's website. Instructions for downloading the models are included in this book.

This book is designed to be followed from beginning to end. Each chapter presents information needed for the next chapter.

New in Version 8

"Gamestudio/A8 can render almost twice as fast as A7, especially scenes with many portals, animated actors and shadows. It's script compatible to A7 and A6, except for projects using the physics engine. This is new in A8:
All editions: nVidia PhysX® subsystem for rigid body physics and raycast vehicles; improved editors; improved content import workflow; accelerated dynamic shadows; unlimited terrain size; improved publish process; overlay windows; trigger regions; 2D particles; new sprite types for vegetation.
Commercial Edition: accelerated bones animation, new network library, extended network functions, shader-based bitmap processing.
Pro Edition: portal renderer, shader compiler, instancing."
Conitec 2011 - Information from Conitec website.

LINK FOR UPDATING VERSIONS

http://manual.conitec.net/newfeatures8.htm

EDUCATIONAL EDITIONS

"For developer teams or for education, multi-seat Team Editions are available. They can be installed on a network server or on a given number of PCs. All members of the team must use the software for the same project or for learning purposes, and may not use it for separate projects or outside the team or classroom. For a Game Programming course use our 25 lesson curriculum with an exit exam at http://tutorial.3dgamestudio.net.
The Team Editions are based on the Commercial or Pro Edition, but don't include the license to publish and distribute games. For this, an additional single edition is required. Team Editions for 3 or more seats at a fraction of the normal edition price can be ordered in the online shop or by email to info (at) 3dgamestudio.net. Students can upgrade their team editions to personal full editions at a reduced price."
Conitec 2011 - Information from Conitec website.

ROYALTIES

"As owner of any Gamestudio single edition you can freely publish and distribute your applications. You don't need to pay royalties, you don't need to show credits, you don't need to ask for permission. There is only one exception. It's illegal to use Gamestudio for games that propagate genocide against a certain group, race, nation or religion existing in today's real world."
Conitec 2011 - Information from Conitec website.

Chapter 2 - **WED Editor**

Open the WED Software

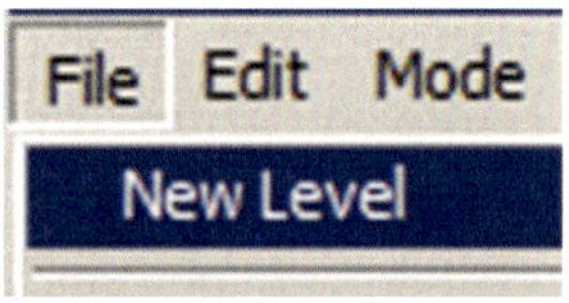

1 CLICK on FILE - NEW LEVEL

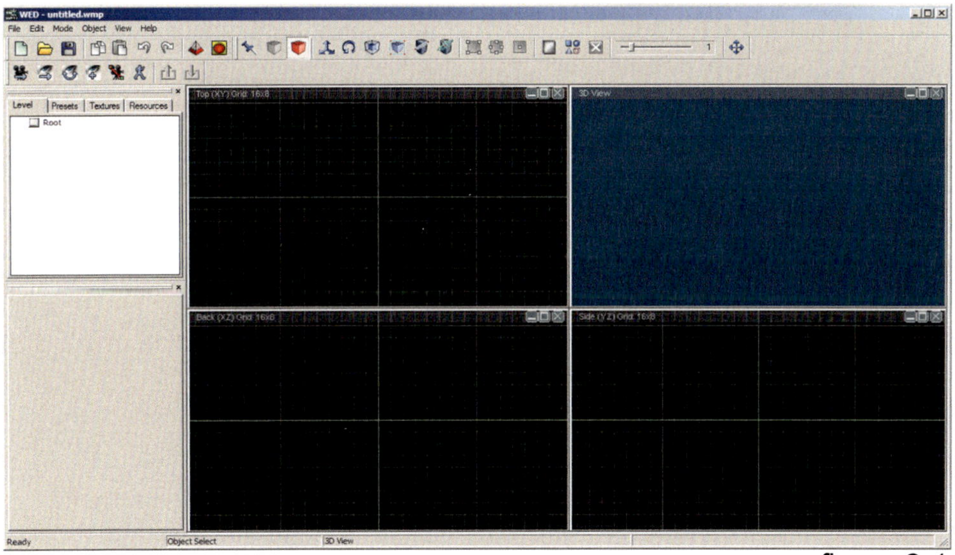

figure 2-1

The NEW icon also opens a new level.

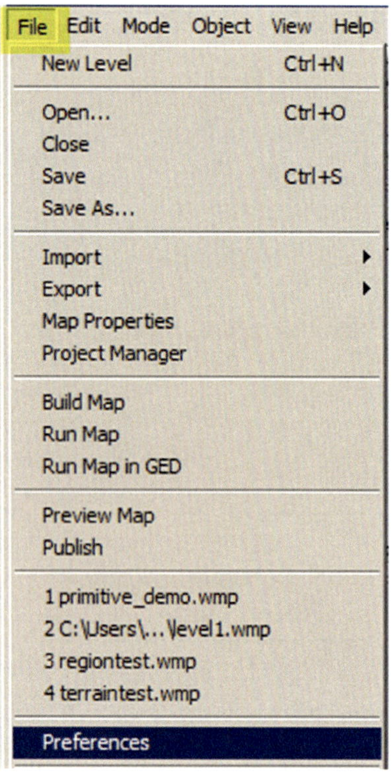

figure 2-2

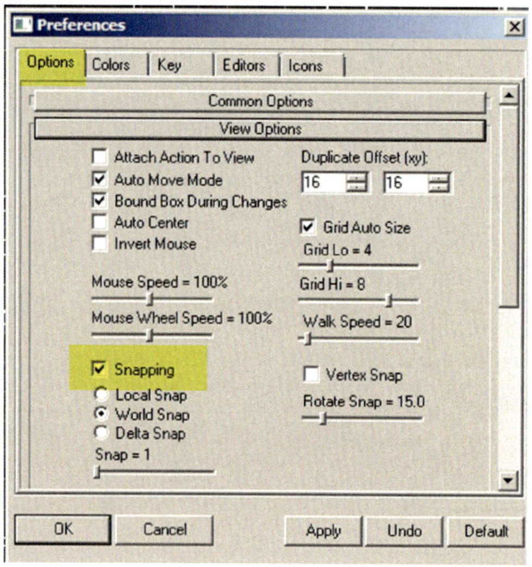

Check Snapping figure 2-2

2 Click on File ➔ Preference➔ View Options and Check Snapping

INFO and TIPS:

At anytime during your building process you need to look up information CLICK on Help - Contents and the Manual appears. Use the search box to find information.

figure 2-2

Other then checking Snapping in the Preferences leave all other settings should be left at their default settings.

INFO and TIPS:

There are different ways to start building a level.
Because this is our first level the information will be presented in a sequence that may not be as efficient as it will be after the first level has been created and everything has been set up. The steps that are presented in this book for a new user will show how and when to add needed components as the first level is created.

After the components have been added creating levels will be faster and easier for the next levels.
For example - this book shows how to create a basic room from an unhollowed block. Then the book introduces adding texture, creating new wad textures and models etc. When you are familiar with Gamestudio and have the new wad textues added and the model script files downloaded then the building sequence will be faster and easier for buildig a level. This book will show how to build a simple room from a block in this chapter and introduce information as we progress and build our level.
In the future when building rooms, first - build the room and size it, you could add a model to guage what size to make the room. That model could be a pre-fab model of a person, a scaled tower, a pre-fab car model etc. The size of the room depends on the game and the elemets being used in the game. After you know what size room you need then hollow the room. Try not to resize rooms after they have been hollowed. Models/players are not introduced until later in the book so we don't have a model to bring into the first room we are making to guage what size to make the room. Also - you want to position models (players) by doorways when you create a doorway to be sure the player can walk through the doorway.

Remember to Save, Build and Run the level often.
Levels should be contained in a sky cube. This book will explain sky cubes in an appendix in the back of the book. The book is starting with the basics.
Be sure to read the appendixes for additional information.
This first room will use the basic components needed to build a room in a level and we will focus on how to build a room, texture a room, and create a second room with a doorway in the first part of this book.

Add a Cube - Make a Room (Add Object)

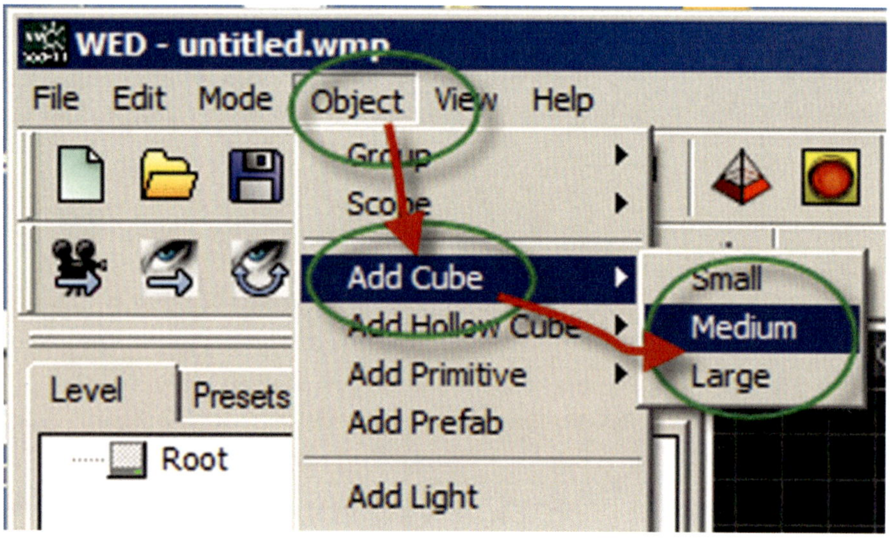

2 Click on Object ➔ Add Cube ➔ Medium

figure 2-2

Info. Or, Add Object icon  on the toolbar will also add a cube to the level.

figure 2-3

3 Click  **Scale** and use the arrows to RE-SIZE the cube.

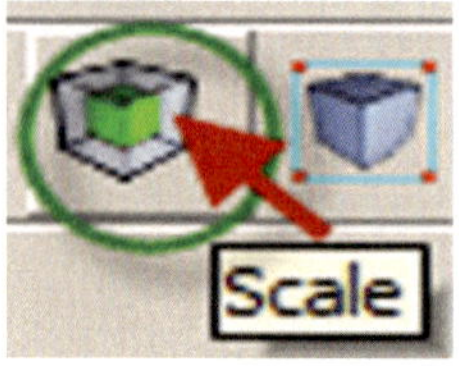

figure 2-4

4 MOVE THE CUBE –  use the three arrows to position the cube on the grid. The cube moves along X, Y and Z planes. Refer to "Primitives"- for a more detailed explanation of positioning 3D objects in space.

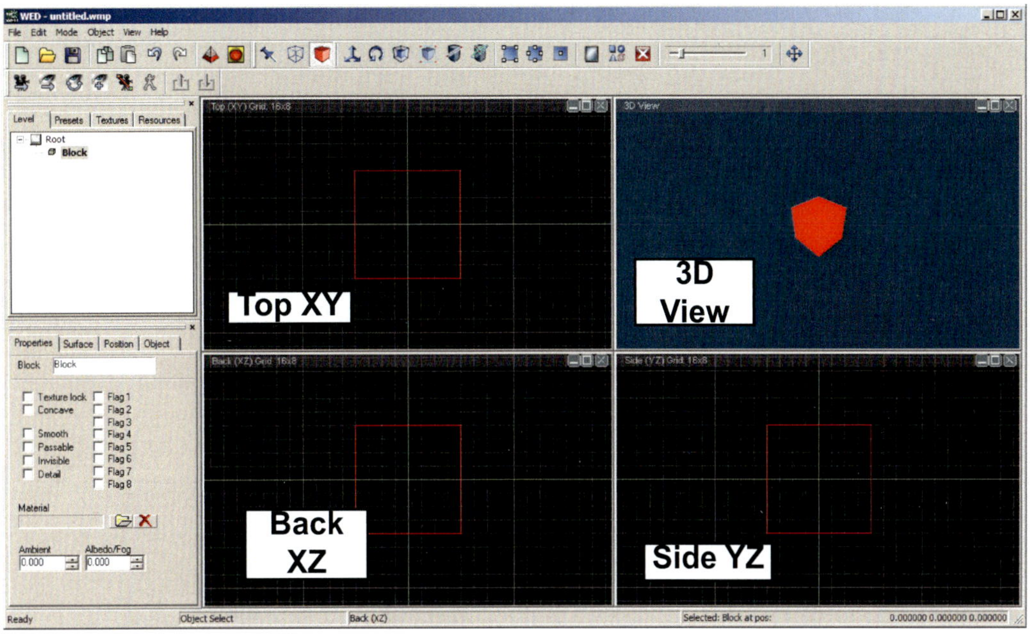

figure 2-5

The Top (XY)Grid represents a view looking down into the top of the cube.

The **(XZ) view shows the Back** view.
The Side view is shown on the (YZ) screen.

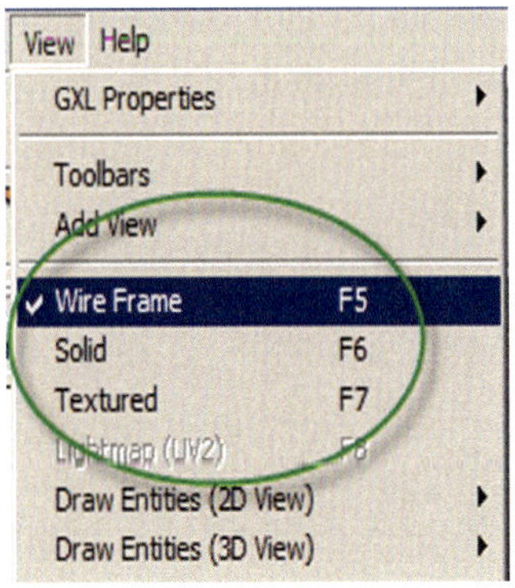

figure 2-6

When the first block loads into the level be sure it is aligned to the grid. **Click Edit - Align to Grid**.

Cube View - The cubes can be viewed in three modes:
wire frame, solid, and textured.

Click on View Tab and scroll down to the Wire, Solid and Texture choices.

Precise Placement of a Cube

On the local Position Tab use the increase/decrease buttons to move the cube on the grid with precise accuracy and click Apply.

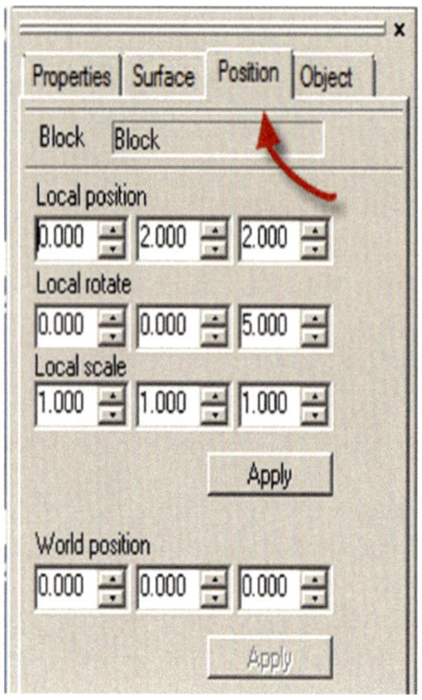

figure 2-7

Next Step -

Make the Cube Hollow

Selecting a solid cube to start this project will create thinner walls on the cube we hollow. Selecting the Gamestudio's existing hollow cubes from the menu creates a cube with thicker sides. It is more difficult to cut openings in thicker walls to pass through to other areas.

1 Click on the newly created block to Highlight it..

2 Click Edit ➔Hollow Block on the menu bar.

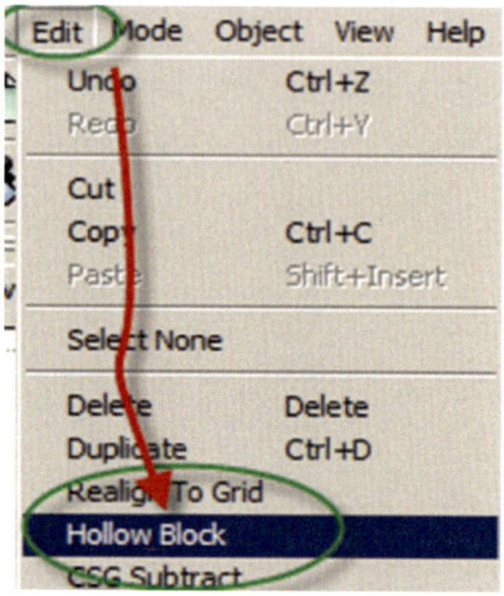

figure 2-8

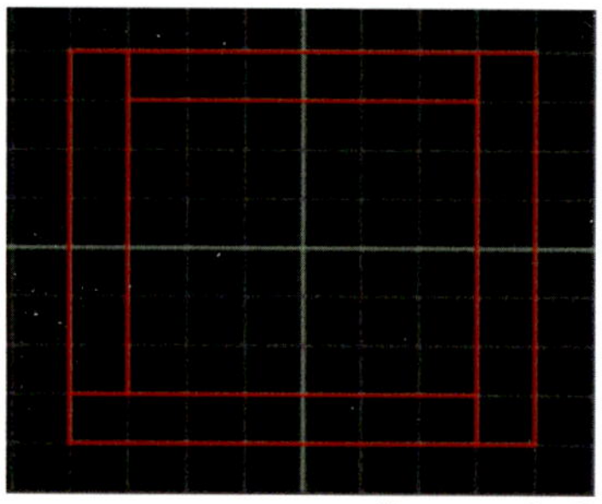
figure 2-9

Instead of a single line defining the cube you will now have doule lines on all edges of the cube.

Level Tab

The Level Tab shows the tree of the current entities and objects in that level. A cube is a block (figure 2-10). When you hollow the Block it becomes a Group with blocks listed under it in the Level tree (figure 2-11)

.

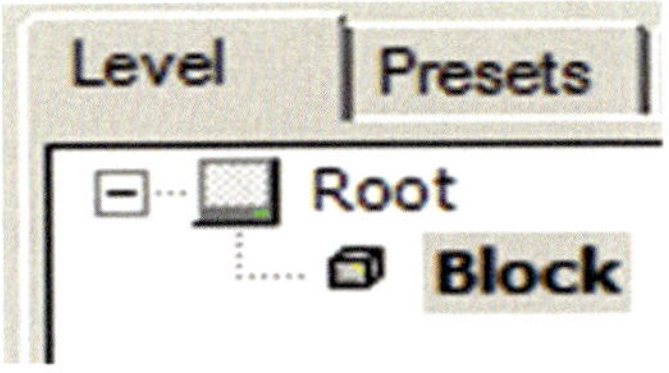

figure 2-10

Cube Not Hollowed

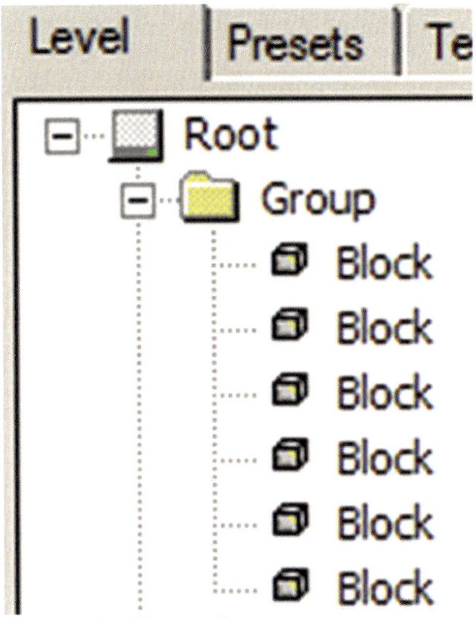

Cube hollowed   figure 2-11

Hollowed Block vs Unhollowed Block

Later, when an opening is created between cubes (rooms) it will be important to use a block (unhallowed cube) to create the opening.

Next Step -

Add Position

Click OBJECT ➔ ADD POSITION on the menu bar to preview the room (figure 2-13). Figures 2-14, 2-15, 2-16 show the position after it is added.

POSITION is represented as a red camera inside the cube. You may move the camera in the room. *Be sure the camera stays inside the walls of the room in all the grid views.*

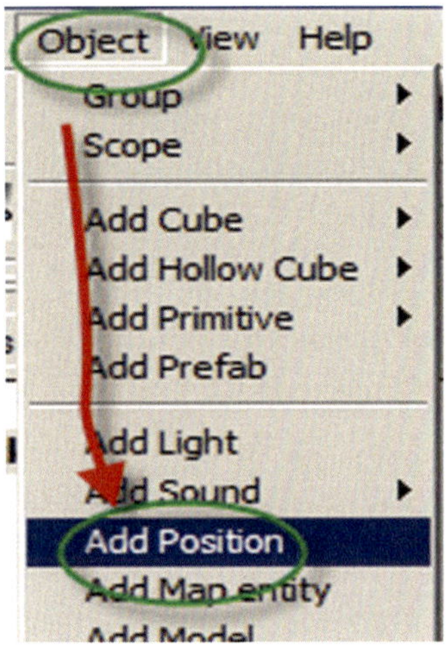

figure 2-13

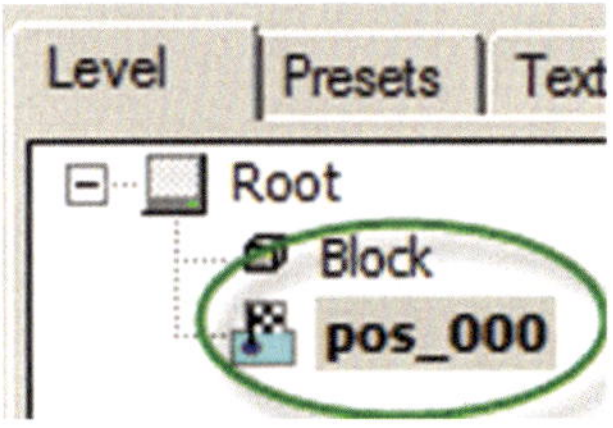

figure 2-14

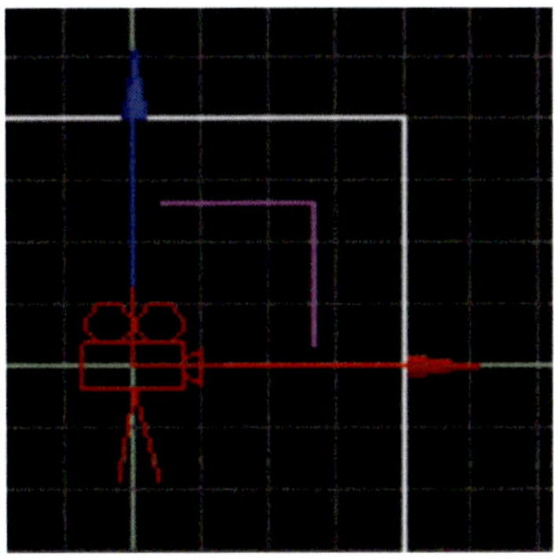

figure 2-15

Add Position

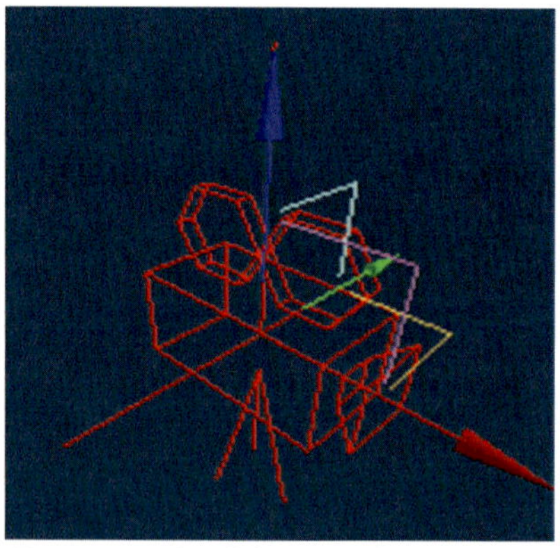

Camera inside the figure 2-16
3D view.

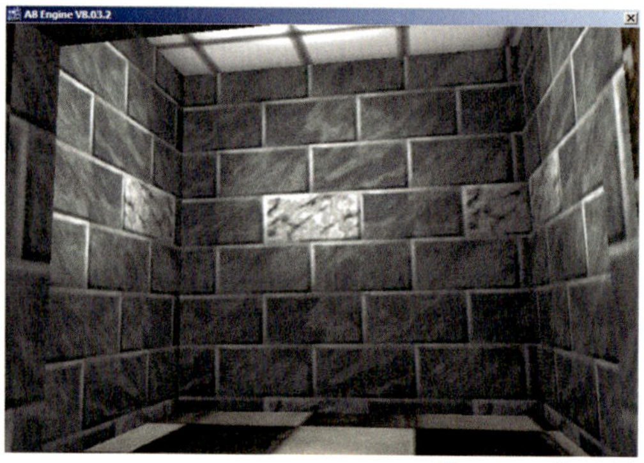

figure 2-17

This picture is from a room that has one light added and a ceiling and floor texture added.

After you build and run the level you are viewing the room through this camera "position."

Be sure to pull the camera down onto the floor. Use the ROTATE tool to position the camera. Then check all the windows to be sure the camera is positioned properly in all the views.

Next Step -

Add Lights

1 Click Object ➔ Add Light

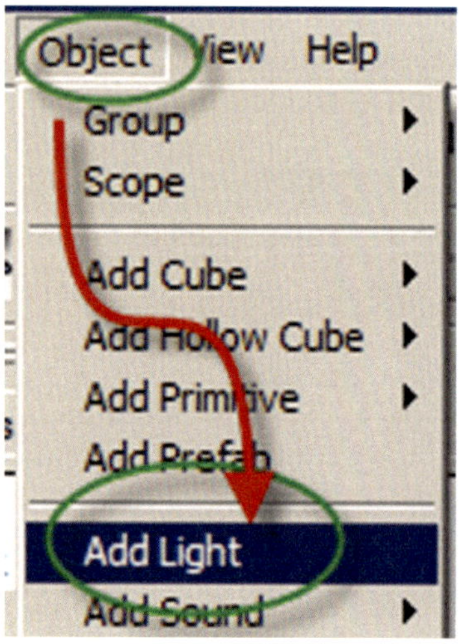

figure 2-18

The light shows up under the Root of the level you are creating.

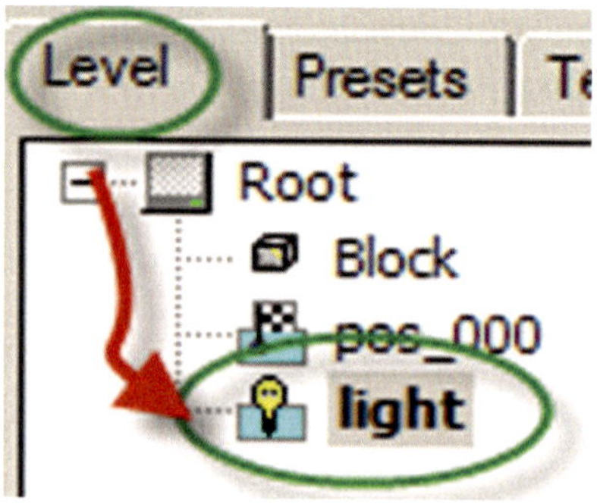

figure 2-19

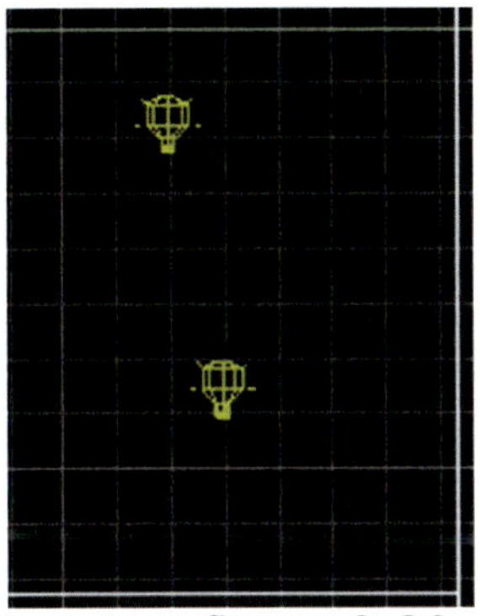

figure 2-20

Lights appear as yellow bulbs in the level.
Be sure to Position the Lights in all four views keeping the lights inside the room walls.

2 **Click on the light to highlight it and make changes.**

Properties Tab

figure 2-21

Under the **Properties Tab** you can change the label "light" to a descriptive name such as "Light under Wheel".

The default range for a light is 300 quants. The default is one quant equals one pixel. 3D Gamestudio recommends that one quant equals one inch.

You can use the buttons on the Properties Panel for each light to increase or decrease the brightness of the colors.

Light color can be changed at any time during the creation of the level. The Red/Green/Blue(Bright) panel allows the user to increase and decrease the primary colors in numeric increments. figure 2-21

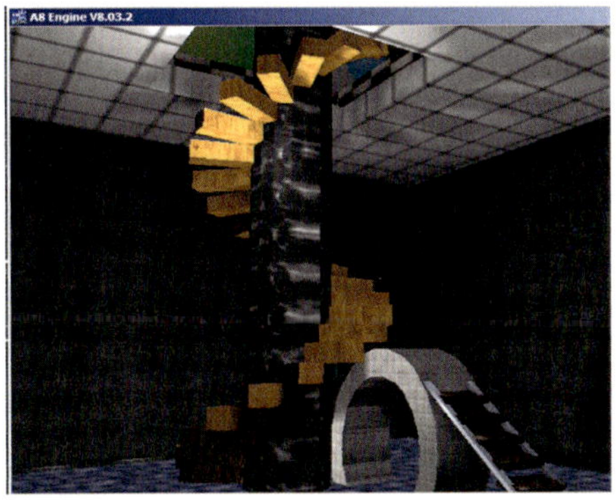

Lighting creates atmosphere in this finished room.

figure 2-22

Add Lights continued

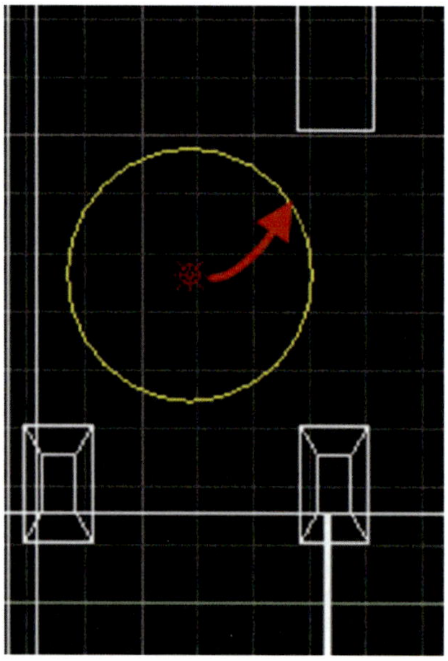

figure 2-23

Figure 2-23 shows the yellow circle which indicates the range of brightness from the light.

Amount of Brightness Radiating from a Light -
2 ways to increase brightness.

1 **Click on the light in the level and activate the Size Tool on the toolbar and use the arrows to increase and decrease the Circle of light around the light bulb.** This method shows the physical distance of the lights projection in the level. figure 2-24

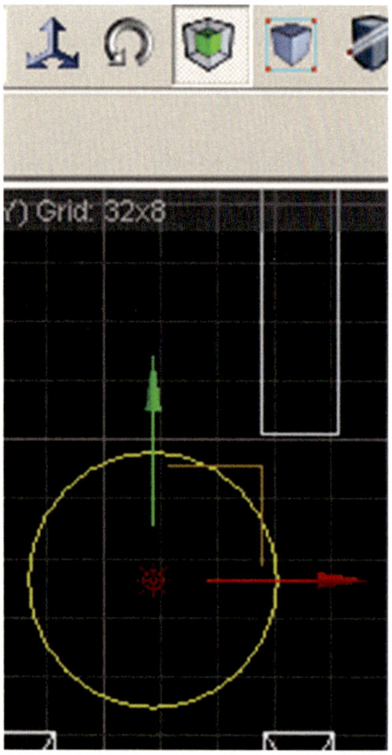

figure 2-24

Position Tab

2 **Use the Position Tab to scalethe size of the light circle and click apply.** figure 2-25

Gamestudio's Light Formula:

Total Light = Ambient Light + Diffuse Light + Specular Light + Emissive Light

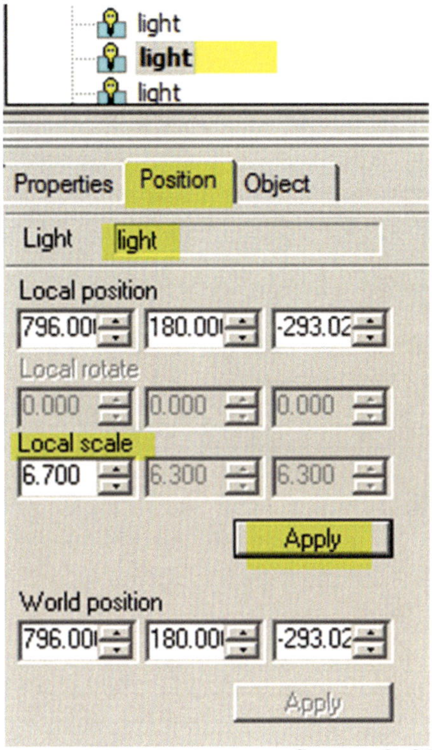

Position Tab figure 2-25

figure 2-26

Completely change the atmosphere of a room by changing the light color.

Changing the Light Color

2 **Click on one of the lights** you've added to your level. This **highlights** the light red and makes it active for the next command.

3 **Click on the rectangle** next to the color settings Red/Green/Blue(Bright)

4 **A color chart pops up.**

5 **Select a color** for the highlighted light. This example is selecting red.

6 **Click OK. The light you selected will now have a colored glow.**

When you click on the light in the WED game level it highlights red (all objects highlighted in the level turn red). The rectangle beside the Red/Green/Blue(Bright) panel will turn the color that the light is projecting. Our example turned the light red and this rectangle shows the color red in figure 2-27.

Changing the Light Color continued

The **Define Custom Colors** panel pops out and allows you to create custom colors and add them to the Custom Colors chart. figure 2-28

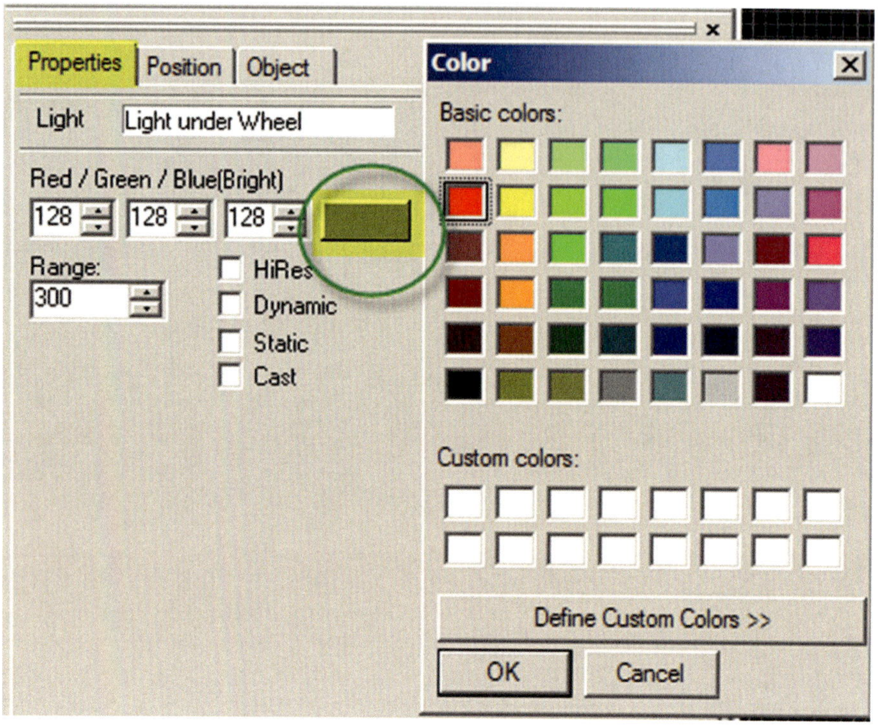

figure 2-27

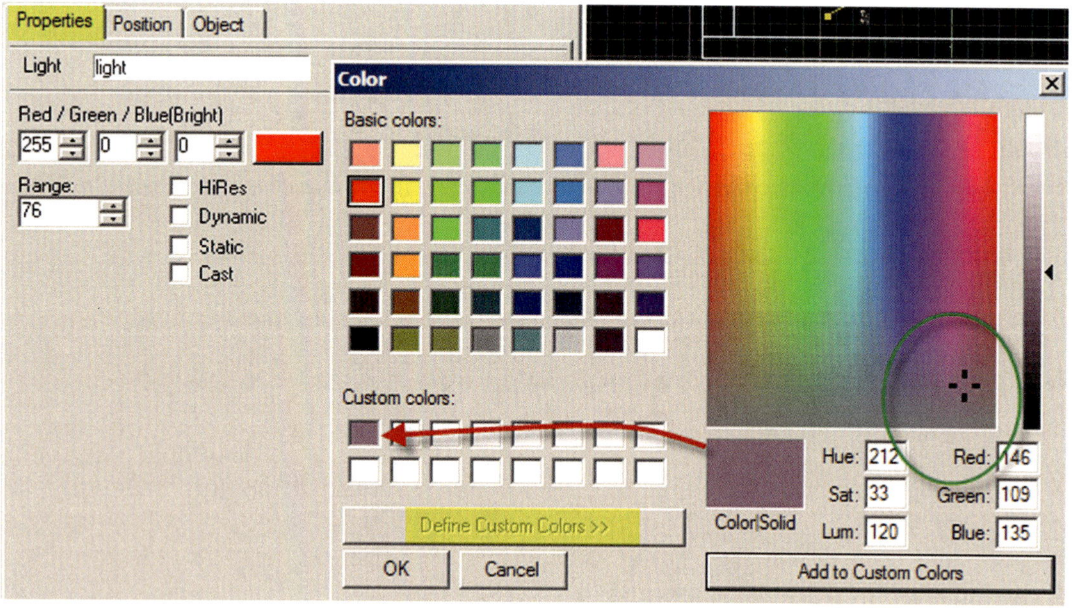

Custom Colors can be created and saved in the WED's Properties panel.

figure 2-28

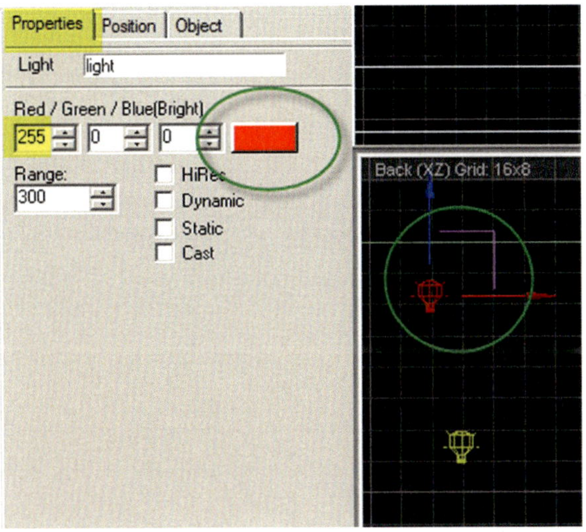

figure 2-29

The rectangle beside the lighting panel not only opens the color pop up window but after changing a light to a colored light it will show what color a light is set to when you click on an individual light in the level.

Figure 2-27 set the light under the bridge red. Figure 2-30 (red light under bridge.

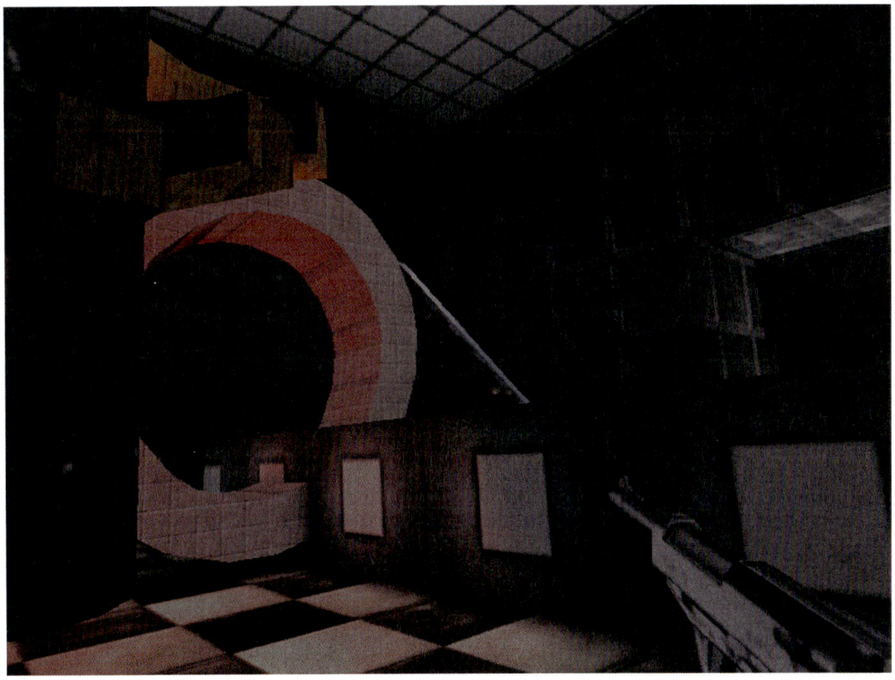

figure 2-30

This is a picture of a finished room inside a game. The light under the wheel has a red glow. The light under the wheel was set to red and positioned directly under the inside of the wheel.

Add Lights continued

Multiple lights may be positioned in a level. Use light to feature walkways or light doorways. Lighting creates the atmosphere in the areas. You may use the default lighting throughout the entire project. You may add lighting as you build or add the lighting at the end of the project. The light parameter has to be set above zero to emit light.

How Many Lights Can Be Used?
Gamestudio's light manager uses a method to calculate which objects are in the "range" of which lights and it generates lists of the lights that are close to every object. You can add many lights to the overall level, and position the lights to highlight certain areas. But only 8 lights at a time are affecting the illuminated area. Lights that are the farthest away from the center of the object will be removed by "light sorting" when more than 8 dynamic lights are affecting the object.

Speed up the Rendering Time
The more lights, the more rendering time it takes to process and this affects the frame rate. It all depends on the number of lights and range of the lights. Range meaning how broad of an illuminated field does the light use. Gamestudio still maintains an 8 light limit but it dynamically switches on and off during the rending process. No more then 8 lights are active during any given time.

Limitations
Because of the limitations of hardware no single Entity, Terrain chunk or Block can receive more then 8 dynamic light sources at the same time.
If any of the above mentioned objects are affected by more then 8 lights then only the 8 most recent lights that have been added will have an affect on the objects.

Next Step -

Save the File

Click File ➔ Save As. Select the location where you want to save the file and name the file. **Click Save**. (At first saving work in the "work" folder is suggested.) Do not include spaces in the file name.

Next Step -

Build the Level

figure 2-31

Click the Build Icon to build the level. (Fig. 2-31) **Click on Build Simple Map. Click Yes to replace with the Default Texture.** (Fig 2-32)

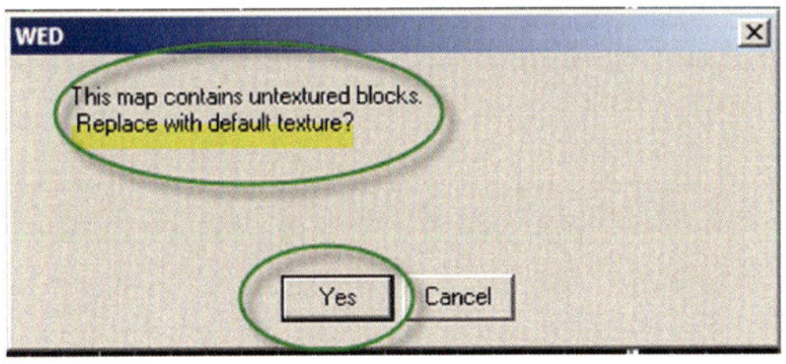

figure 2-32

Map Compiler

If you have a large level to compile it is suggested that you use lower visibility/light calculations to speed up the time needed to compile the level.

Map Compiler

Make adjustments on the map compiler and **click OK**.
The level will automatically compile.

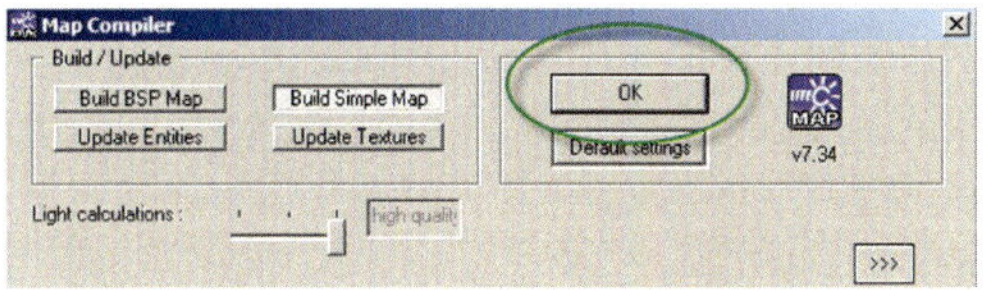

figure 2-33

Click OK to close the Map Compiler Generator.

Next Step -

Run the Level

Click on the Run Level Icon.
After the level runs the created room appears in a separate window.
You are looking at the room through the camera "position" you added.
figure 2-35

If an error occurs check the file name for spaces or errors. Sometimes additional characters will appear after the .wmb file. If this occurs erase additional characters after the extension then click OK. Refer to Appendix F.

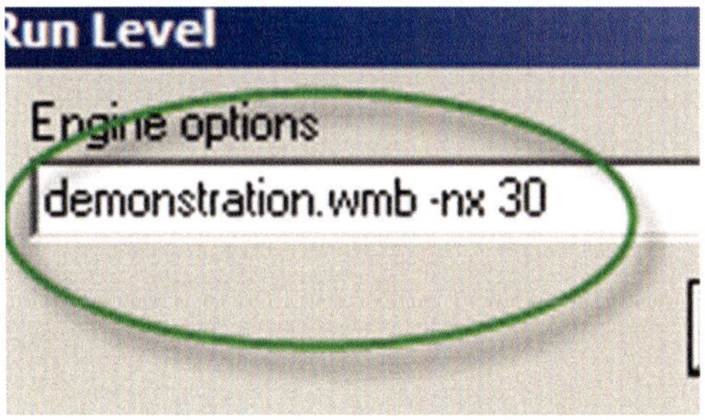

figure 2-34

BUILD converts the map into the .WMB format, adds lighting information and generates the BSP tree, Binary Space Partitioning Tree.

Built, Run and Compiled level.

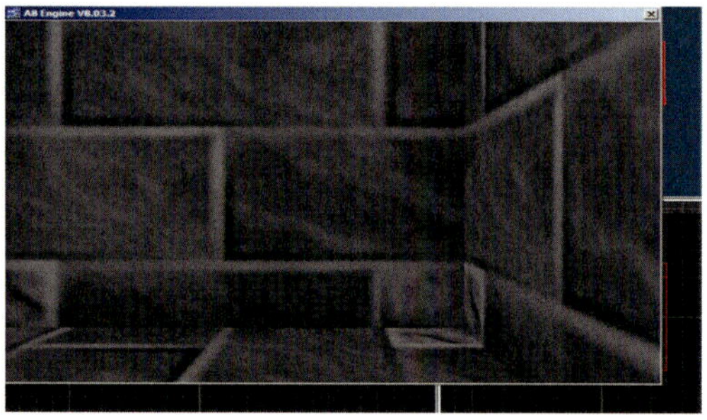

figure 2-35

Separate window appears with the built level.

Move Around the Room

Use the Arrow Keys to rotate around the room, side to side, zoom in and out.
Hold down the right mouse button to move the camera and view the different areas of the room.

Center Your Work on the Screen

While working on your project, sometimes the cubes on the screen move off to the side and out of the Grid viewing area.

Bring the cubes back to the center of your Grid screen- Click on View ➔ GOTO Center. (Centers views to object scope)

Or, **hold down the right mouse button and drag the screen around till you center the image**, Or **press the home key to center your image**.

Next Step -

Add A Second Cube & Create Additional Rooms

1 **Click on the Add Cube icon.**

Or, **Add Object** through the Menu **Object ➔ Add Cube ➔ Large**

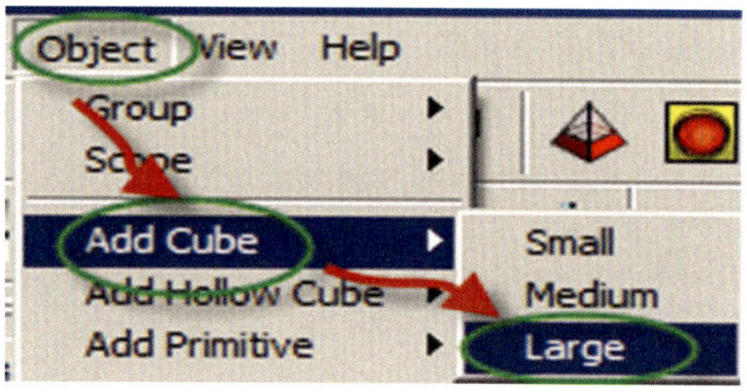

figure 2-36

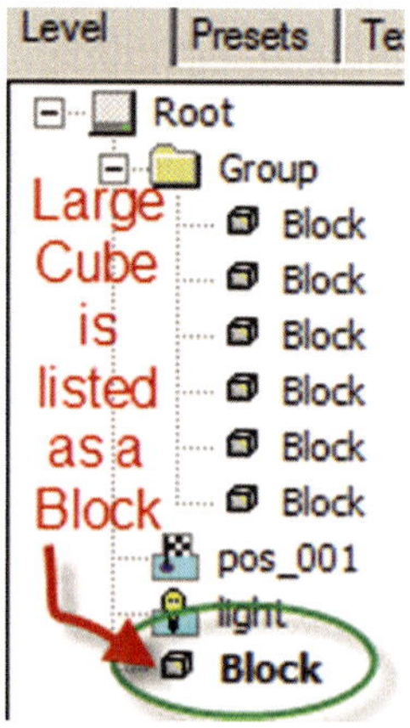

figure 2-37

LEVELS TAB - The first cube is listed as a Group with Blocks representing the six sides. The New Large Cube is listed as an Un-hollowed Block.

2 Scale - Highlight the new large cube by clicking the scale button.

Clicking the scale button changes the green arrow and red arrow. Pulling on the arrows increases and decreases the cube size with the scale button clicked.

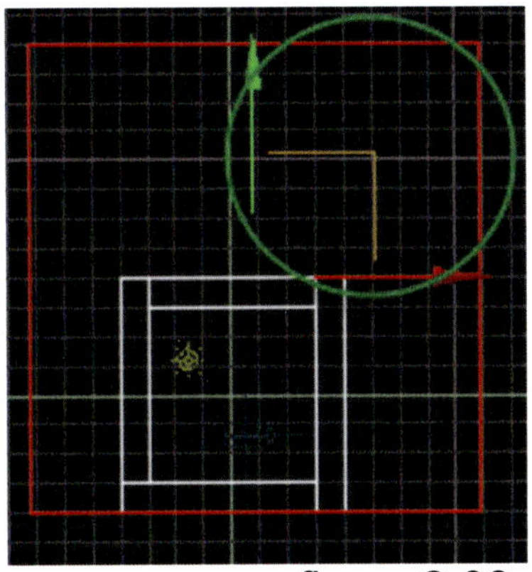

figure 2-38

When a new cube is created and highlighted the Tan Angle with Arrows MOVE the block. The Green Arrow moves the cube up and down. The Red Arrow moves the cube side to side.

In figure 2-38 adding a new cube (Red Box) has placed the large cube over the first smaller cube (White double lined box).

3 Click Edit ➔Hollow Block on the Menu Bar. This hollows the cube into an open room.

MOVE-

4 With the large cube highlighted - Grab the tan angle and move the new large cube. Line up the edge of the large cube to the side of the first cube.

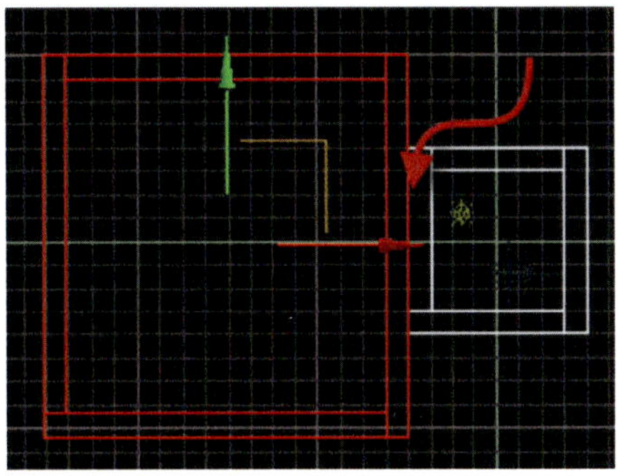

figure 2-39

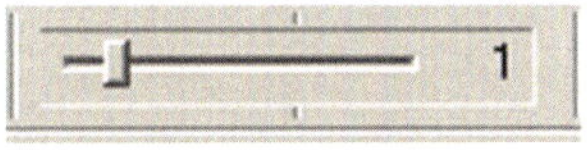

Grid Scale figure 2-40

5 Modify the grid scale for a tight fit. The default is 1. Slide the scale to zero.

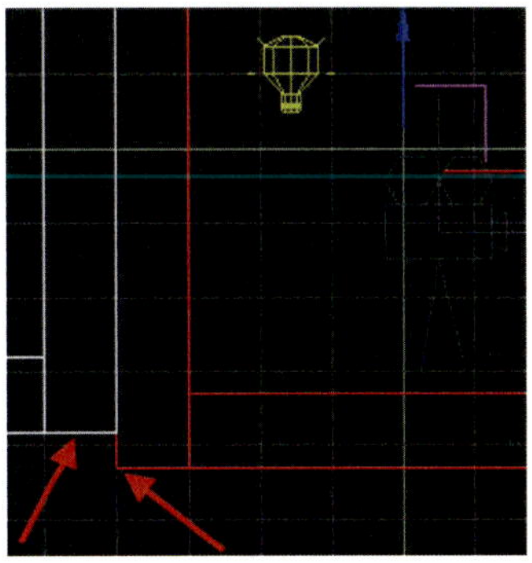

figure 2-41

6 Align the cubes floors, pull in tight for a close alignment. Use arrow keys.

BUILD THE LEVEL

RUN THE LEVEL

File ➔ Save the Level ➔ Click on Build ➔ Click Yes to replace with default texture ➔ Click OK on Map Compiler ➔ Click OK to close Map Compiler ➔ Click Run ➔ Click OK on Run Level.

Level Tab

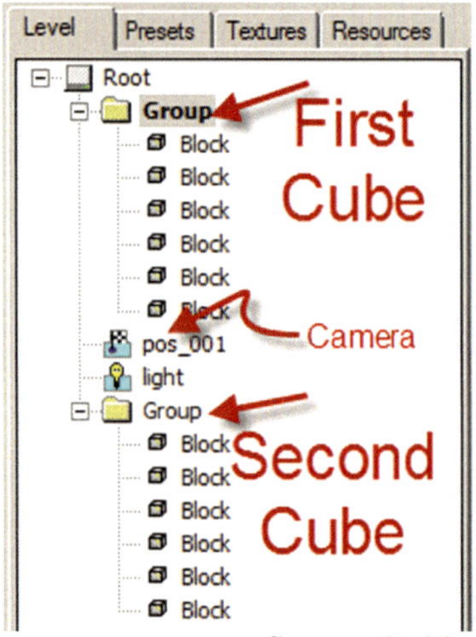

figure 2-42

Info. Don't use extremely narrow, elongated, or acute blocks. Always try to design your map with as few surfaces as possible.

Info. Use the snap to grid function when possible. Align Blocks to each other. Perfectly vertical and horizontal edges in all the views compile and render faster.

Keep your map small. Blocks render more accurately the closer they are to the center of the map. If you need a large map - use blocks for structures like buildings, and use entities for the details such as columns or posts.

Next Step - Now that we have two rooms created and aligned beside each other we need to add an unhollowed cube to use as a cutter to create an opening betwen the rooms.

Create An Opening

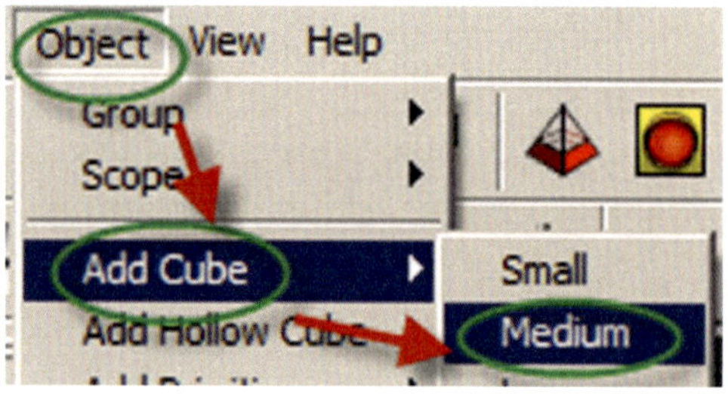

figure 2-43

1 **Click on Object➔ Add Cube ➔ Medium**. This cube will be placed between the rooms.

2 **Click on the newly created cube.**

3 **Click on scale and scale the new cube down to a size that will fit between the two existing rooms.**

4  **Click move and use the arrow keys/or drag to move the newly created cube between the rooms.**

figure 2-44 shows the new "red" block being pulled down into position. Wire View is being used.

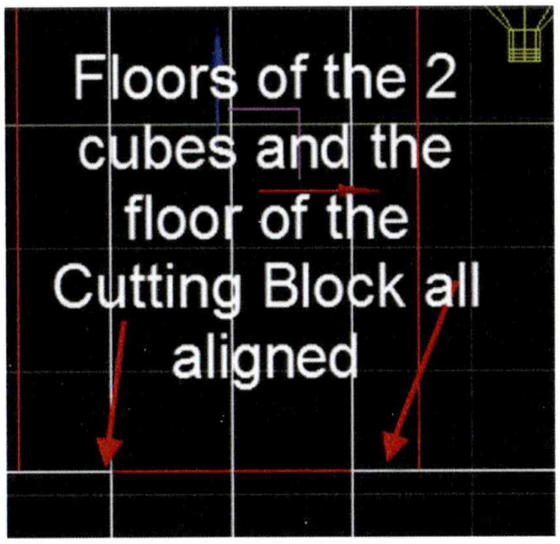

figure 2-44

5 **Position the third cube down into the room to create an opening. (doorway)** Check multiple views of the block to make sure it is positioned properly.

6 **Modify the grid scale for a tight fit. The default is 1. Slide the scale to zero.**

7 **Zoom in** by moving backwards with the roller on your mouse. Use the right mouse button to move around. Make sure in the Back XZ Grid Screen the new doorway cube is on the room's floor line. Fig. 2-44.

8 Position the bottom of the CSG Subtract cube on the actual floor of the cubes. NOT the very bottom line in the wire view.

9 With the Third Cube highlighted red - positioned between the two main cubes (rooms) ready for **CSG Subtract**. Be sure to check the cube position in all the views.

Next Step -

CSG Subtract

You can highlight the **unhollowed block** by clicking on it in the 3D view, or you can click on the block in the Level Tab.

A single block on the levels tab is a cube/block that has been added and not hollowed. figure 2-38 shows the unhollowed cube as red.

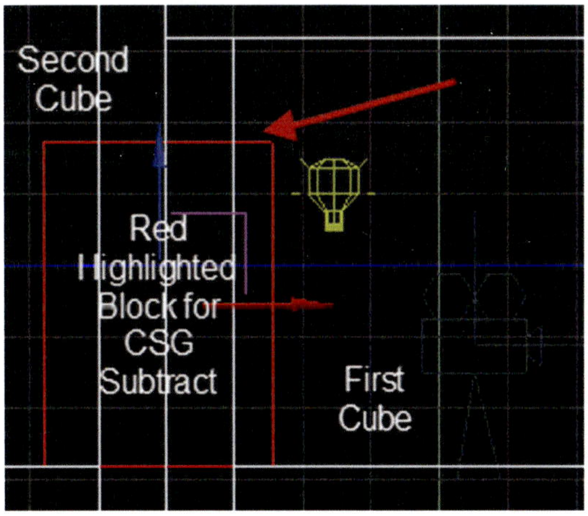

figure 2-45

Figure 2-45 shows first cube and second cube with the red highlighted CSG block in between ready to create an opening.

CSG Subtract continued

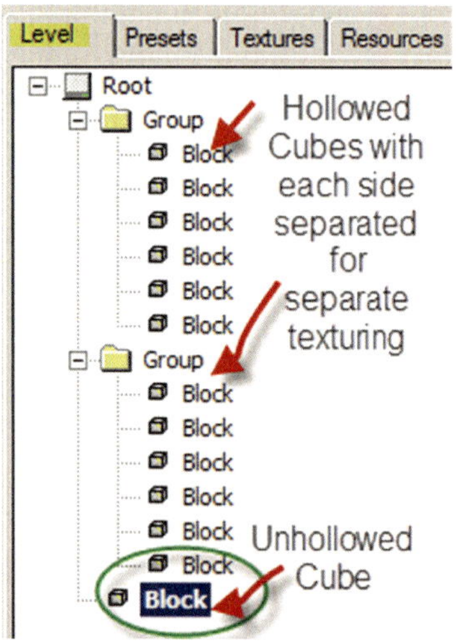

figure 2-46

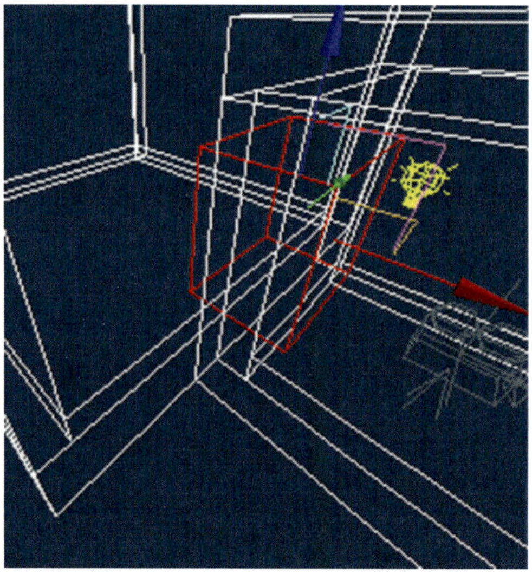

Before CSG Subtract figure 2-47

1 With the Unhollowed Block highlighted and positioned between the first and second cubes **Click on edit on the meu and click on CSG Subtract.**

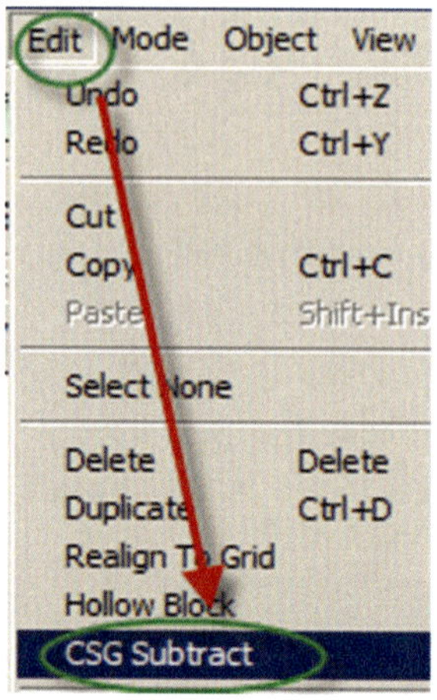

figure 2-48

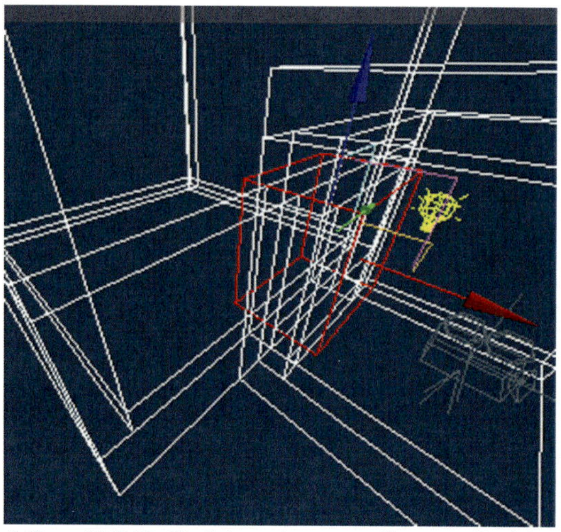

After CSG Subtract figure 2-49

After the CSG Subtract the opening has been cut out. There are more white lines in the wire view which represents the newly created opening sides.

2 **Click File - Save**

3 **Click on build the level ➔**

Click yes replace with default texture. ➔ Click OK on Map Compiler. ➔ Click OK to close Compiler.

4 Run ➔ Click OK on Run level

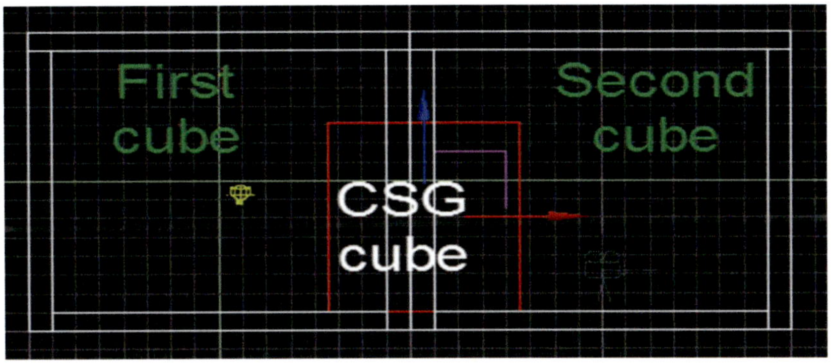

figure 2-50

Before CSG Subtract. Third unhollowed cube positioned precisely between first two cubes. Lined up at the floor. Zoom into the view all the way then position the subtract cube on the lines of the floor. Be sure to delete the CSG Subtract cube before compiling. When sizing the CSG Block be sure it does not extend into the ceiling or floor. Check all views.

5 **Click on the CSG Subtract block and delete the block.**

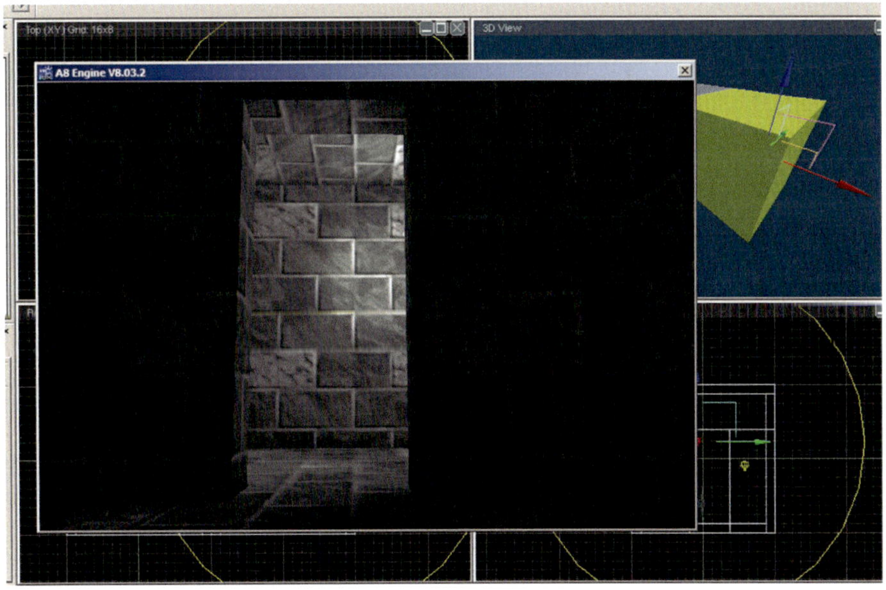

figure 2-51

After CSG Subtract. View from inside the cubes after compiling and running the level. The CSG Subtract cut an opening between the cubes. Default texture applied.

Chapter 3 - **Textures**

Standard.wad Textures

TEXTURES - are used to make objects look more realistic. You are applying a visual "picture" to the object. Textures are created in external software programs. Gamestudio's textures are referred to as WADs. **Paint.net** is a free software program that can be used to create textures.

Info. There are different methods to use when texturing. This book will first show how to texture the entire block by scoping down into a group. The selected group first HIGHLIGHTS RED then after clicking Scope Down it TURNS WHITE. Select an entire block within the group, such as a roof or wall. The texture will be applied to ALL SIDES of the selected block within that group.

Later, this book will show how to modify textures and texture each separate surface. Gamestudio comes with a basic default texture. Other textures are available within the software by opening the standard.wad file under textures.

Next Step -

Open standard.wad

1 **On the Textures Tab: Click on DEFAULT.WAD and open it. ➔ Right Click on the DEFAULT. WAD block ➔ Click on Texture Manager. figure 3-1**
2 **Click on Add WAD** figure 3-2
3 **Click on STANDARD.WAD** figure 3-3
4 **Click on OPEN** figure 3-3
5 **Click OK.** At the left of the Grid views under the **Textures Tab scroll down to open the standard.wad**. Figure. 3-4

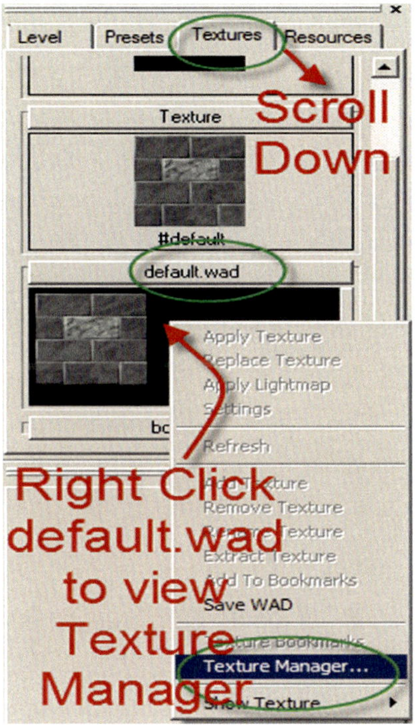

Texture Tab figure 3-1

The default.wad contains the grey brick default texture.

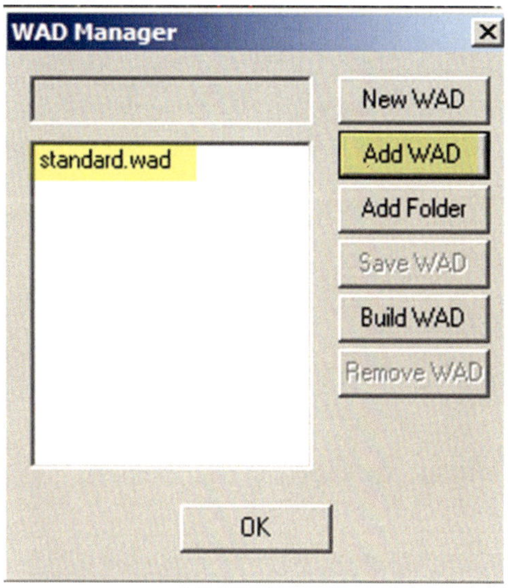

Wad Manager figure 3.2

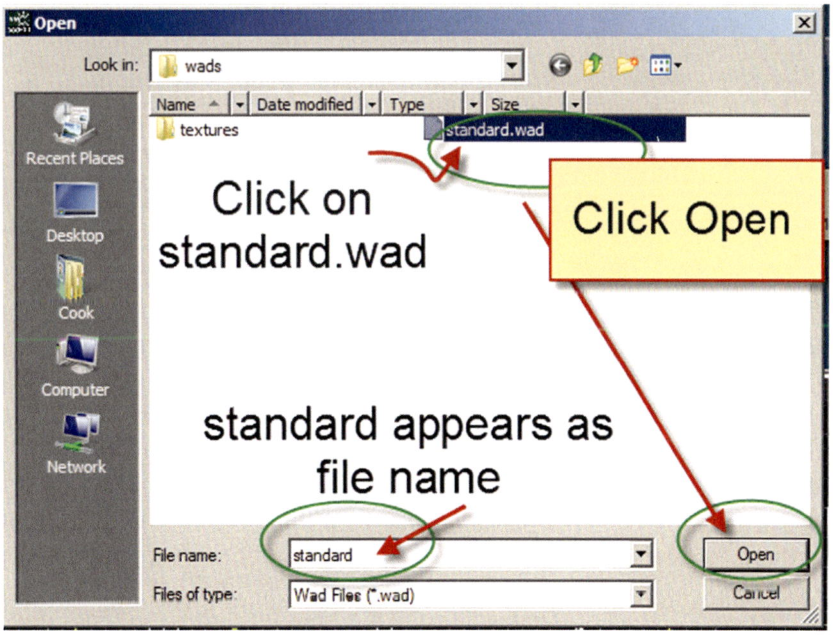

Creating and Opening a Standard.wad file. figure 3-3

Standard.wad Textures continued

This new standard.wad has many new textures. The first five textures are animated and used for water surfaces. The sky textures are applied to the Sky Cube. Appendix B covers Creating a Sky Cube.

Info. Save Textures in the WADS folder in the gstudio 8 folder in the program files.

64 bit computer - x86/gstudio/wads

Next Step -

Apply a Texture

1 **Highlight one of the cubes.** 3-4, 3-5

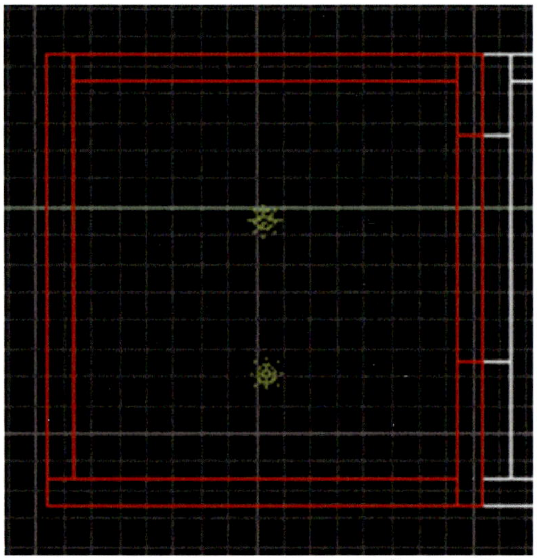

figure 3-4

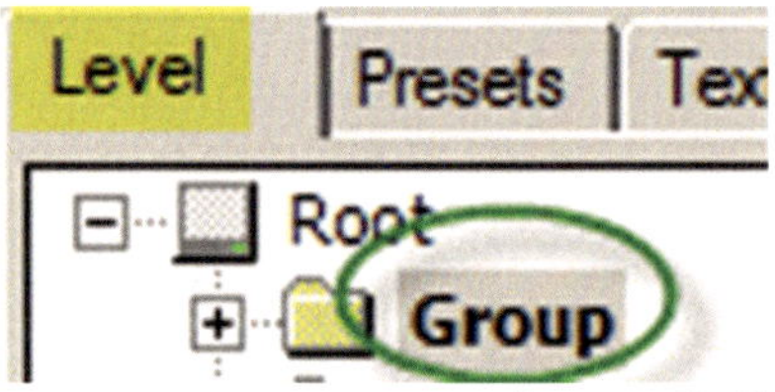

figure 3-5

2 **To apply the same texture to the entire cube - go to the texture tab and double click on a texture - or Right Click on the texture and Click Apply.** figure 3-6

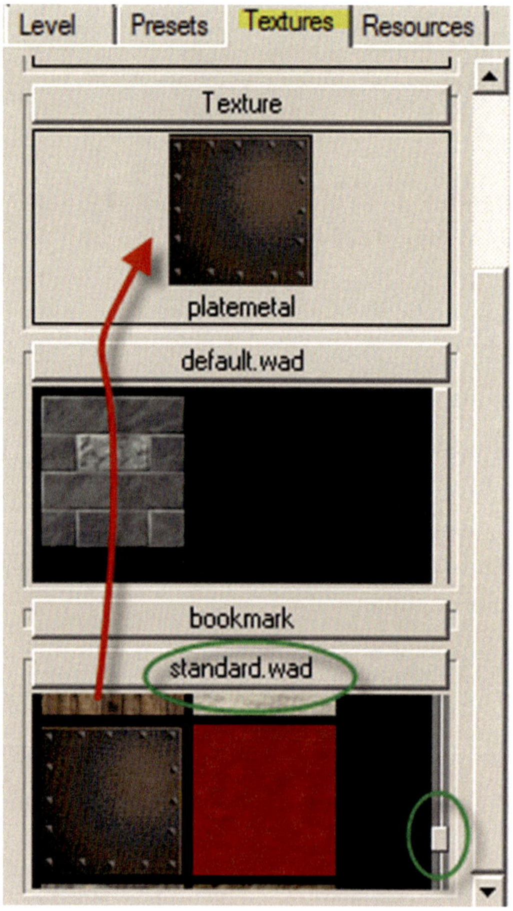

figure 3-6

Platemetal texture has been applied to the entire cube in our example. figure 3-6

Two Cubes Textured

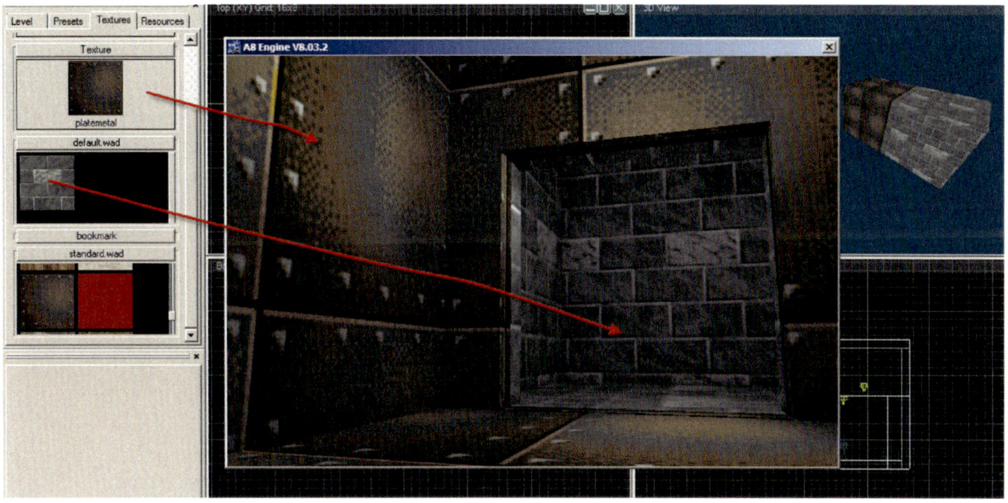

figure 3-7

After texturing the entire room (outside and inside) the level has been BUILT and RUN. The Platemetal texture is applied to the nearest room and the room on the other side of the doorway still has the default texture. This level has multiple lights added to the rooms for printing purposes. Use the arrow keys and the right mouse button to navigate in the built and run level window.

Next Step -

Texturing Individual Blocks of a Group

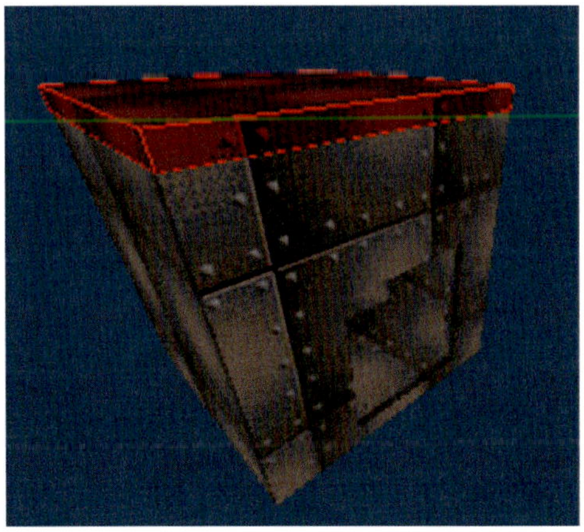

figure 3-8

Scope Down

1 **In the 3D View Click on the room you just textured.** It highlights red.

2 **Click on Scope Down**

3 **Click on the roon's roof.** The roof is highlighted red. fig. 3-8, 3-9

Texturing Individual Blocks of a Group continued

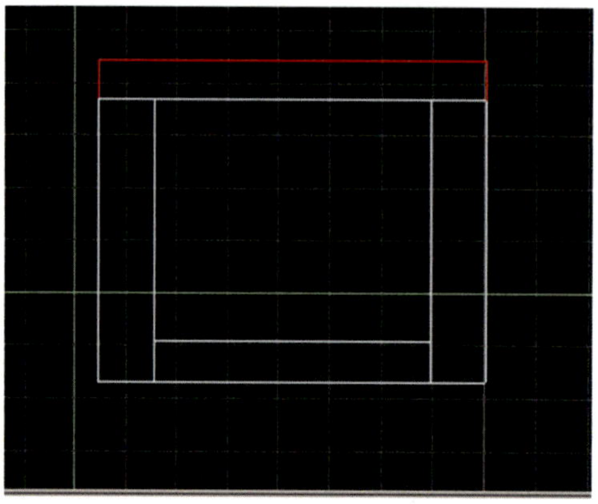

figure 3-9

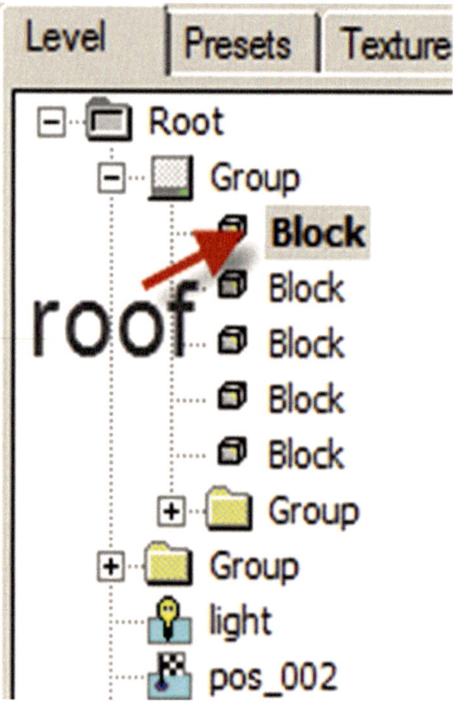

figure 3-10

Info.

If clicking on the roof of the cube in the 3D view (or the other views) does not highlight the roof red then you can highlight the roof by using the Level Tab. Determine which room is the newly textured room by clicking on Group in the levels tab. Watch the 3D view window to see which cube highlights red. Then open the Group and click on each individual Block untill you highlight the roof. fig. 3-10

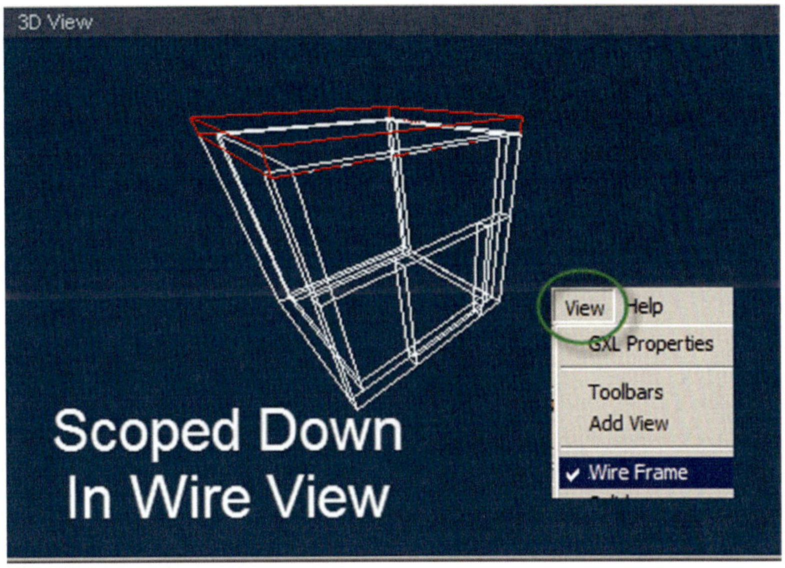

3D View figure 3-11

4 **Click on View ➔ Wire Frame -** this gives a clean image in the 3D View to apply texture. You can see through the block and determine exactly what is highlighted.

The roof of the cube is highlighted to start the texturing process. This selects one Block out of the Group.

Scope Down continued

SCOPING UP AND DOWN is the quick and right way to work on separate units in the WED level.

REMEMBER to first click on the group you want to texture then click on scope down and highlight which block you want to texture.

The rest of the chapter on texturing will assume you know how to click on the group and scope down to highlight the block you want to texture.

Pages 36 thru 41 will demonstrate texturing the individual surfaces of the Block within the Groups.

Texturing Individual Blocks of a Group continued

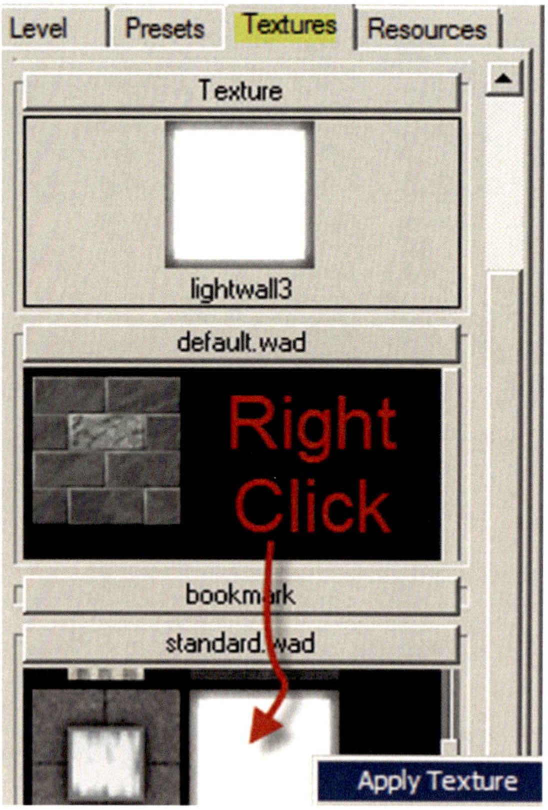

figure 3-12

5 **Scroll down the standard.wad panel to select a texture for the roof.**

6 **Click on a Texture, ➔ Right Click ➔ Click on Apply.**

7 **Scope Up**  **to leave scope view.**

8 **Under View on the Toolbar Click on Textured to view the finished cube with the texture applied.**

9 **Then switch back to the wire view.**

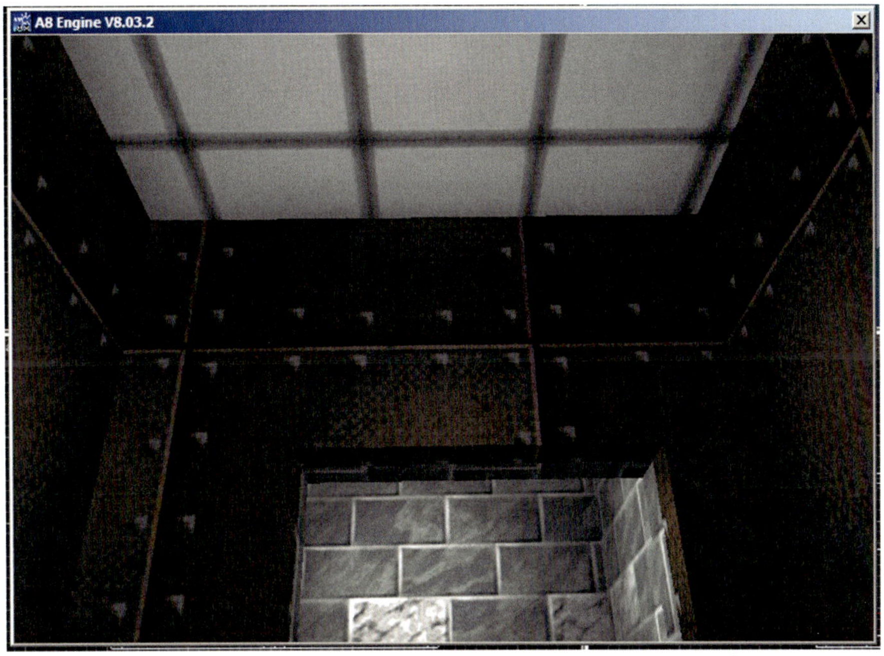

Ceiling of the room textured to look like it has frosted glass panels. figure 3-13

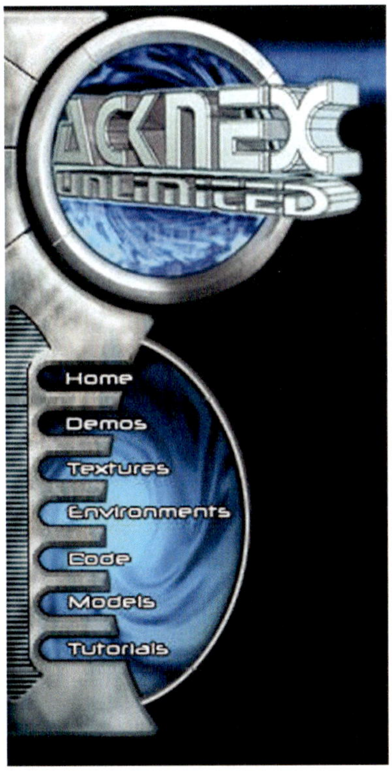

figure 3-14

Sources for information and artwork.

Where to get more textures -

Info. At the Gamestudio website there are many textures available to download. Look in the ACKNEX magazine online at the following website.

http://au.conitec.net/

3rd Party Tools, Artwork & Resources can be found at:

http://www.3dgamestudio.com/

Texturing Individual Blocks of a Group continued

Add texture by switching back and forth between the Levels Tab **and the Textures Tab. Figures 3-15 and 3-16.**

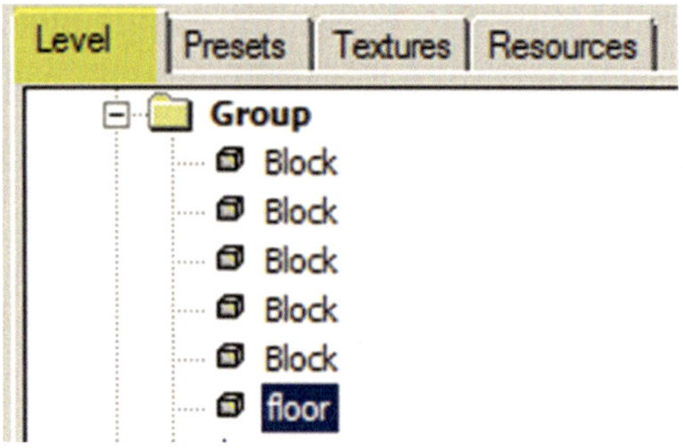

figure 3-15

1 **Go to the Levels Tab and open the GROUP under the Root. figure 3-15**

2 **➔ Select a BLOCK under the GROUP to texture by highlighting the block.**

3 **Switch back to the Textures Tab ➔ Double Click a texture to apply to the selected block.** figure 3-16

<u>Double Clicking</u> on the texture panel is another way to apply texture to a highlighted section of a Group/room.

This example is texturing the floor with a checkered pattern.

There are numerous ways to work on the objects. By switching back and forth between the Textures Tab and the Levels Tab you can quickly texture a cube. (group with blocks) The individual Blocks will be highlighted under the Levels Tab.

figure 3-16

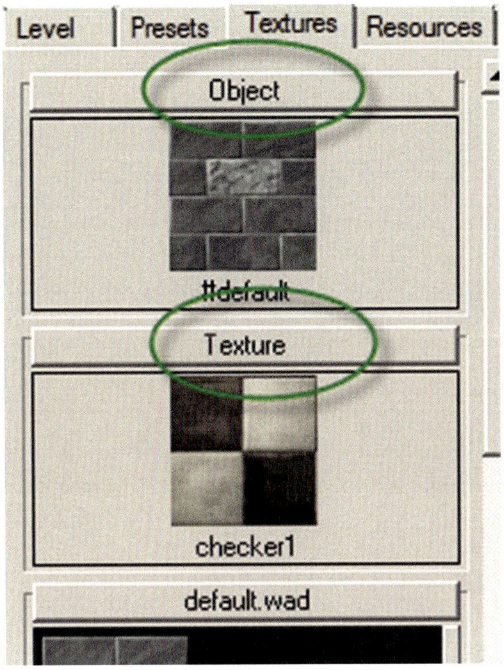

figure 3-17

After a surface has been textured the Object section appears in the Texture Tab. When you click on a textured surface in one of the four views the Object window will show the texture that is on that surface. Figure 3-17 shows the current texture that is loaded and ready to be applied in the Texture window. It shows the Default Texture in the Object window.

For all non-visible surfaces - bottoms or non-visible sides the level will compile faster if they aren't textured. It saves texture memory.

Bookmark Textures

Open the BOOKMARKS PANEL. Right Click on the TEXTURES PANEL with the texture you want to bookmark loaded then Click on ADD TO BOOKMARKS and the Texture in the Active Texture Panel will be added to the bookmark textures.

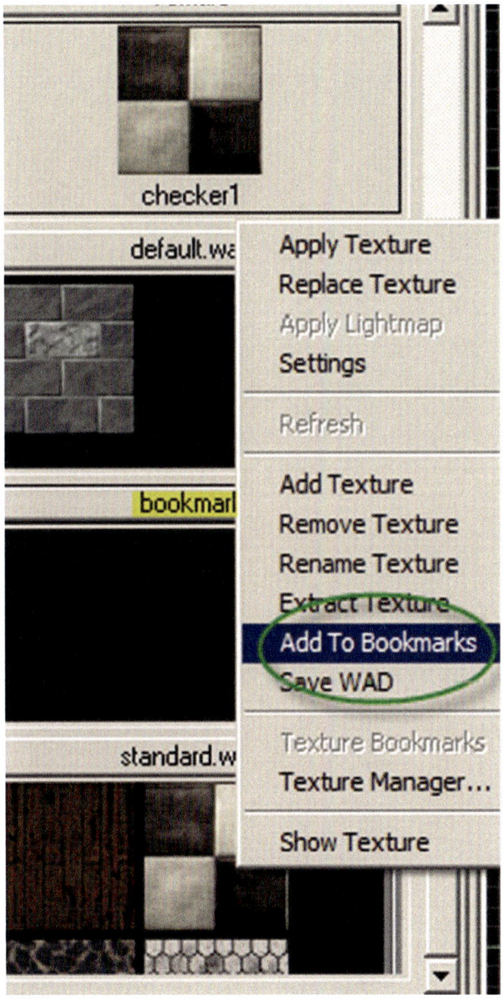

figure 3-18

Next Step -

Scaling a Texture

In figure 3-19 the floor texture pattern is too large for the size of the rooms.

figure 3-19

figure 3-20

In figure 3-20 the floor pattern has been scaled down to 0.2 and the pattern has been angled 45 degrees. (Surface Tab)

1 **With the floor in one of the rooms/ block highlighted click on the Surface Tab.** figure 3-21, figure 3-22

2 **Lower the X and Y SCALES to make modifications**. In this example the X Scale and the Y Scale have been lowered to .2 which decreases the size of the block pattern. figure 3-16

Info.

To highlight a single Block - On the Levels Tab - Select the Group (Cube) then click on each block watching the Views to see which Block highlights - then with the correct Block/ surface highlighted apply a texture.

Clicking on the individual blocks on the screen view also highlights the block and prepares it for texturing. When an individual Block is highlighted the Properties/Surface/Position/Object panel appears. figure 3-21

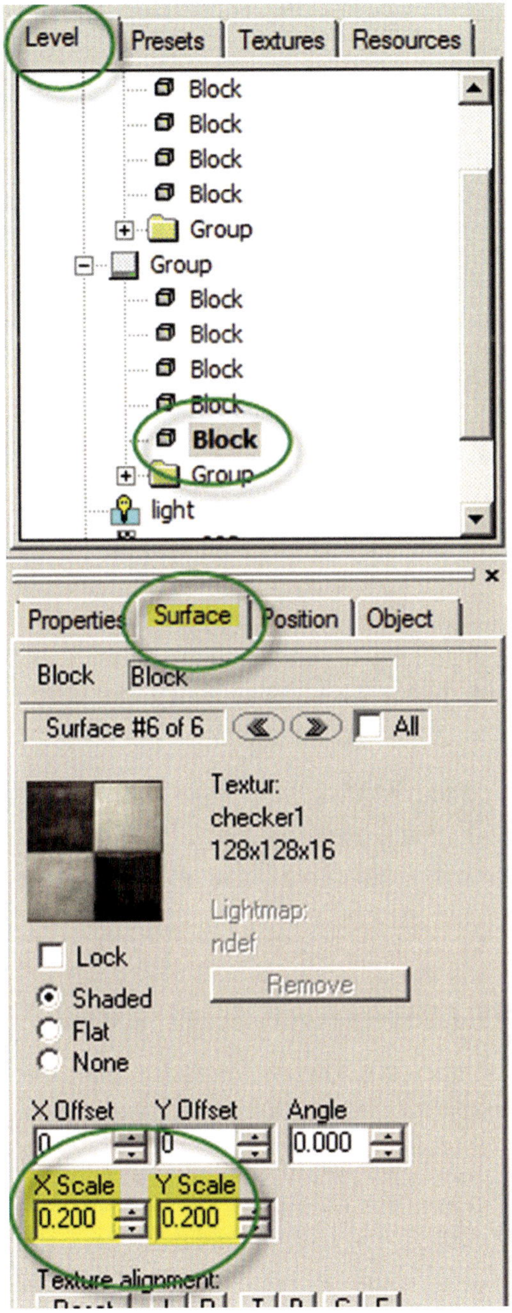

figure 3-21

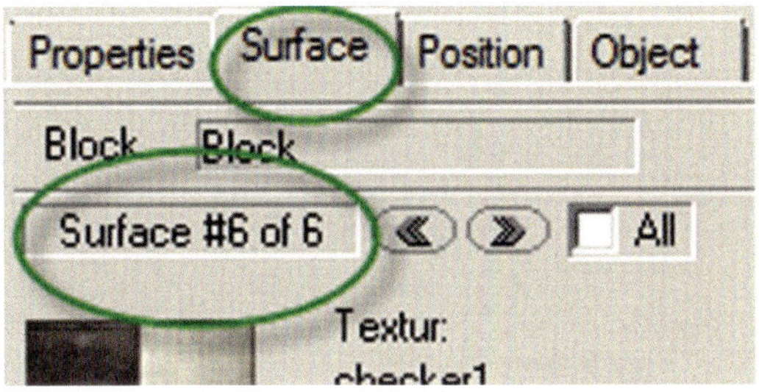

figure 3-22

The SURFACE TAB shows the individual blocks/surfaces as a number. The floor is block number 6. figure 3-22

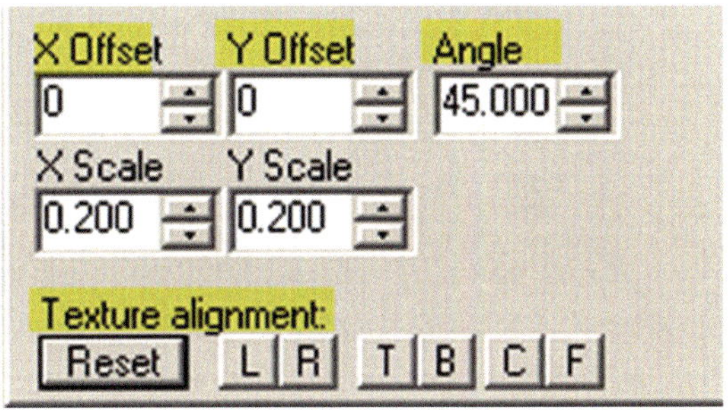

figure 3-23

Texture Alignment

L = Left Alignment
R = Right
T = Top
B = Bottom
C = Center
F = Fit

In figure 3-23 the front room floor pattern has been scaled 0.2 and angled 45 degrees. The X and Y offset and the Texture Alignment can adjust texture patterns so texture patterns line up at corners and floor and ceiling angles. Adjusting texture patterns makes the level look more realistic.

Texture Alignment - when texturing a door for example, the wad texture for a door can be applied to the door cube - click on **F for fit** and the door pattern will be sized automatically. You can first try the Fit command then see if the texture needs adjustments.

figure 3-24

One room with the floor pattern scaled down. The opening between the rooms still has the same texture as the walls. The back room floor has not been scaled.

Matching the Texture Size throughout the level

Don't change the scale settings from the first floor's surface. Apply the texture to the cutout and the other room's floor to obtain a consistent pattern.

If the patterns do not align properly with a full block aligned to the wall, or ceiling and wall blocks don't match at the corners the **OFFSET SCALE** moves the texture back and forth and side to side to align the patterns. The X and Y Scales can also be changed for the finished pattern alignment. (Play with the settings - you will see the textures moving in the 3D view.)

Also, the **TEXTURE ALIGNMENT** buttons quickly move the textures for proper alignment.
By **LABELING the GROUPS AND BLOCKS** it is easy to click on each named block and apply the same texture and settings throughout the level.

Next Step -

Labeling Groups and Blocks

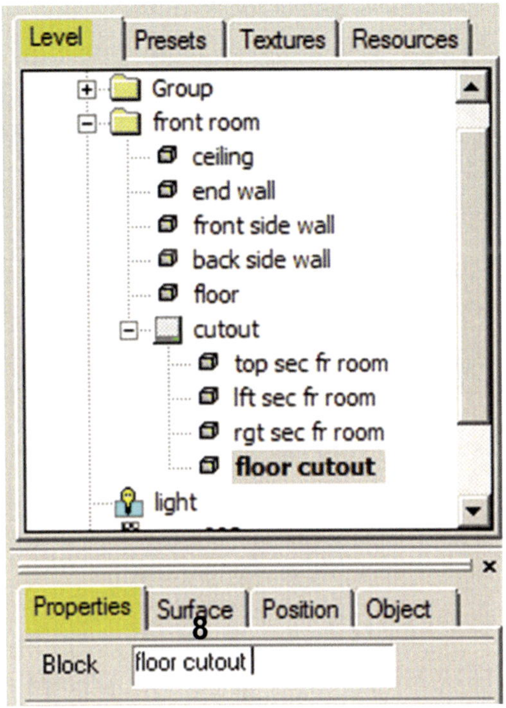

figure 3-25

It is easier to texture if each component added to the level is labeled to reflect the environment being created. Ex: Front Room, Passageway, Red Room etc.

1 **OPEN a "Group" in the Level Tab** check the 3D View and the other views to be sure the group you have selected is the one you want.

2 **Click on the "Properties Tab"** In the example figure 3-25, the Block name for the "floor opening" has been changed from the generic "block" to "floor cutout".

3 **Click on each "Block" under each Group** and using the **Properties Tab label the different blocks**.

Texture Commands

Add Texture - adds a PCS, BMP or TGA texture to the WAD.

Apply – applies the texture in the textures window to all the faces of the selected object. You can also apply the texture by "double clicking" on the selected texture.

Texture Lock – locks a texture to an object if you want to move the object.

Rename – renames the currently selected texture.

Remove – Moves the texture from the WAD.

Add to Bookmarks – adds a texture to your bookmarks.

Save WAD – Saves the WAD file.

Selecting each Block's Separate Surface for Texturing

The first example in this book applied texture to an entire group. The second example applied texture to an entire block. These are quick methods to texture rooms and surfaces. The previous example textured a cube's floor with a tile pattern.

To detail the WED environment and apply texture to make objects look more realistic each of the block's sides can be textured separately. The following example will use the "floor opening" section between the two rooms.
Figure 3-26 shows the floor section with the same texture as the walls on all surfaces of the "floor opening".

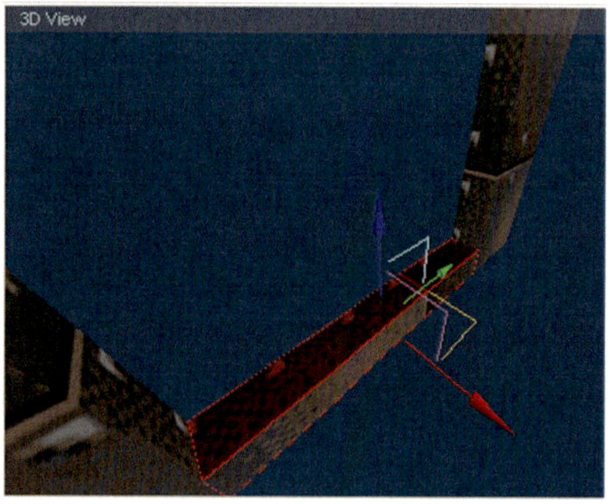

figure 3-26

3D View screen showing the cutout in the "textured view" with the top surface of the floor cutout highlighted and ready to be textured.

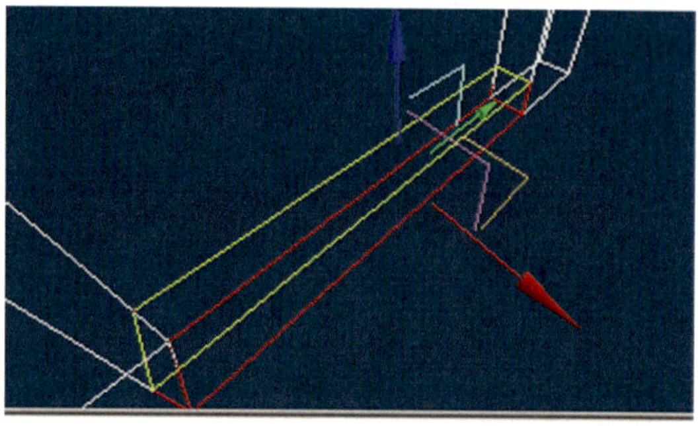

figure 3-27

Wire View of the cutout in the 3D View Screen. (On the toolbar CLICK VIEW and CLICK WIRE)

Surfaces

Shaded - This is a normal texture with a shadow map which provides static and dynamic lights.
Flat - Use this texture for outside, it does not have a shadow map. Flat is shaded to the angle position of the sun.
Sky - The texture is a sky texture by default if the texture name begins with 'sky'. Use the sky texture for a sky box that surrounds the entire level.
Turbulence - This is the default texture if the texture name begins with '*'. Use this texture for liquids. It is liquid and warping and used for water or lava.

None - Surface won't be rendered.

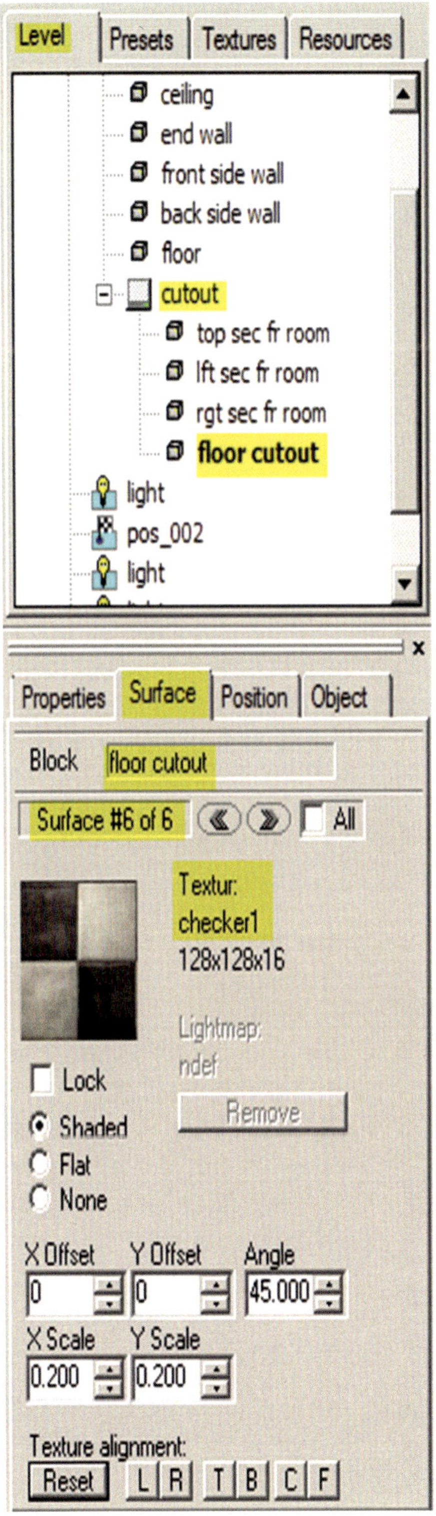

figure 3-28

Level Tab and Surface Tab information:

Group - Cutout (Group is the cube or room. The Group has 6 parts; ceiling, floor, 4 walls.)

Block - Floor cutout (Block is one of 6 sections of the Group or room. This Block is the Floor section of the larger Group "cutout".)

Surface - #6 of 6 sides (The floor of the Group was surface 6 and the top of the floor section for this cutout is #6. You can rotate through the Surfaces and watch how the numbers coralate to the yellow highlighted surfaces.)

Texture - Checker 1 (On the Textures Tab the checkered floor pattern is selected and shows on the Surface Tab.)

Figure 3-27 shows the Wire View of the “floor opening”.

Figure 3-28 shows on the Surface Tab the Block “floor cutout” SURFACE #6 of 6. This is the TOP surface of the “floor opening” block.

Surface #6 or 6 is shown highlighted in **figure 3-28**. The Block is highlighted and the active surface ready for texturing is highlighted yellow.

Texturing a Surface

1 **On the LEVELS TAB - Double Click on the "floor cutout" block under the Group named "cutout" - or - Scope Down in the 3D view into the level and click on the Block you want to texture.** This example is texturing the top floor surface of the opening between the two rooms. (We first highlight the correct BLOCK within the GROUP.)

2 **Click on the TEXTURES TAB** – select the floor texture to load into the Texture window. Our example is the black and white tile texture, checker 1.

3 **Click on the SURFACE TAB – ROTATE THROUGH THE SURFACE NUMBERS until the TOP SURFACE of the cutout floor is shown as YELLOW in the highlighted Block in the 3D View** (6 of 6)– **Wire View.**

4 **DOUBLE CLICK on the highlighted surface on the View Window to apply the texture - OR - RIGHT CLICK on the TEXTURE window under the Texture Tab (you have previously loaded the texture you want to apply into this texture window) Click apply and texture surface 6 of 6 on the "floor cutout".** Fig. 3-28

5 **Click on View on the Toolbar and change the View to Textured View**. The 3D window should look like Fig. 3-29 when you zoom into the room in the 3D View. scoped down. Fig. 3-30 shows the floors of the two rooms textured and the floor surface of the opening also textured. They all blend together as one floor pattern.

figure 3-29

Sides of a Block that are not seen do not need to be textured. The level will compile and run faster if you leave these surfaces untextured. This example has the side and bottom textured because we first textured the entire Group.

Floor texture applied to only the TOP SURFACE of the block "floor cutout".

Finished Textured Floor throughout the Level

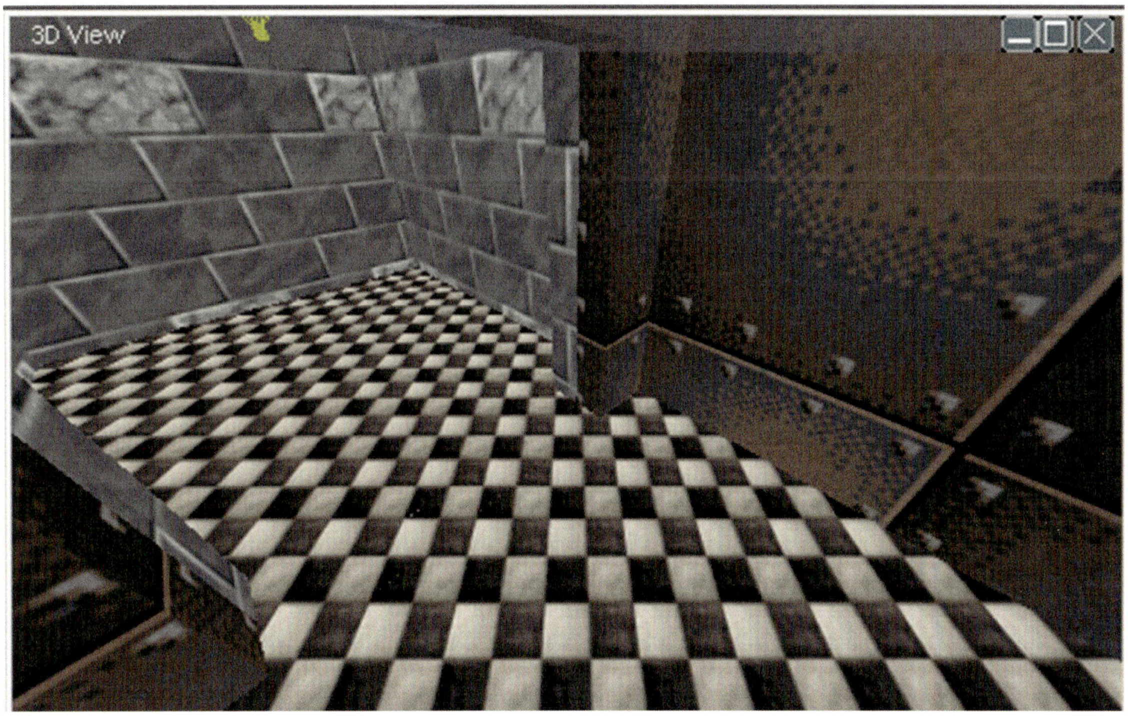

figure 3-30

Figure 3-30 shows the floors of both rooms and the "cutout" opening. All surfaces are textured with the same "checker 1" texture. All surfaces are angled at 45 degrees and all surfaces match up. To perfect the texturing use the Offset and the Texture Alignment to move the floor pattern for a more aligned look.

The platemetal walls in the front room should be scaled and aligned. The ceiling pattern also needs to be scaled.

Some people don't use the 3D view window to make changes. Just be careful and double check your other views and the level tab to be sure you are working on the correct surface.

Scaling and Aligning Textures

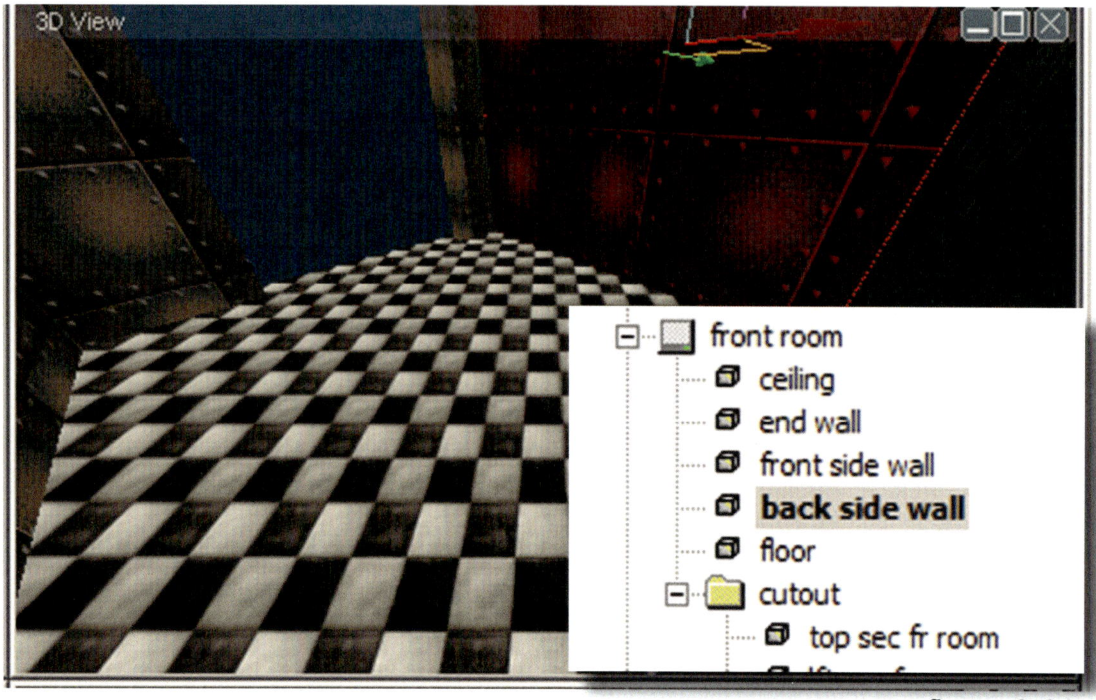

figure 3-31

1 **On the LEVELS TAB highlight the section you want to texture, scale and offset align.**

2 **On the TEXTURES TAB select the texture you want to texture the section.**

3

ZOOMED INTO the 3D View to watch the scaling process.

4

Click on the LEVELS TAB with the section highlighted (this is showing the back wall of the front room)

5 **USE THE ARROW KEYS TO SCALE AND ALIGN THE TEXTURE.** As you change the scaling and alignmet the 3D view highlighted section will move and you can visually watch how the texture changes.
The back wall plates start at the bottom with a full plate, unlike the other walls where the plates are cut off near the floor.

Downloading Texture Files from the Internet

1 **Create a folder on your desktop and name it "Textures."**

2 **Download Texture files** from http://au.conitec.net.

3 **Extract the Downloaded Files to your "Textures folder".**
The zipped files will make their own folder in your textures folder.

4 **Next navigate to the Gamestudio installation folder. Start ➔ My Computer ➔ Local Drive (C:) ➔Program Files ➔Gstudio7 ➔WADS.**

5 **Place the downloaded textures from the desktop folder "Textures" into this WADS folder.**

Info: Save custom and downloaded textures in the Gstudio8/ WADS folder.

Additional Textures cannot be added until the standard.wad textures are installed-pages 28, 29, 30.

Info: If you are using 64 bit Windows Vista operating system gamestudio program files could be in program files x86.

Creating a Folder for your Custom Textures

Paint.net. After creating custom textures they can be placed into the standards. wad file or they could be placed into a separate folder "custom textures". The following instructions show how to create a folder for the custom textures within the GStudio WAD folder.

1 **Navigate to Program Files ➔ GStudio7 ➔ WAD**

2 **Open the WAD folder**

3 **Create a New Folder named "custom_textures"** This new folder will hold your custom textures.

Paint.net - Creating a Custom Texture

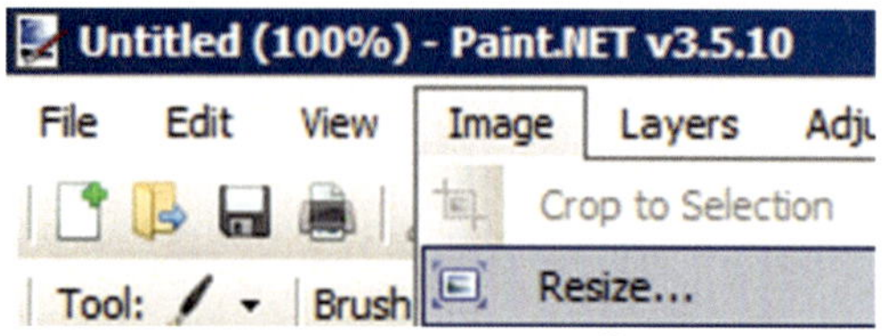

figure 3-32

1 **OPEN paint.net software ➔ CLICK IMAGE ➔ RESIZE**

2 **ENTER 128 x 128 on the Height and Width Pixel Scale ➔ CLICK OK**

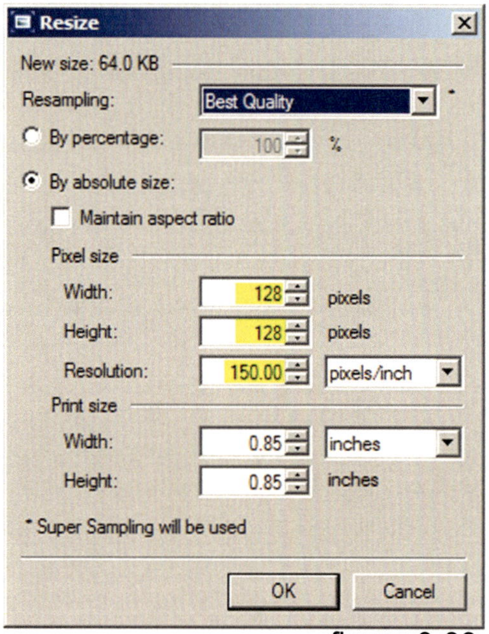

figure 3-33

3 **Create a Custom Texture with Paint.net or Import artwork for your custom texture onto the 128 x 128 canvas.**
This example is using some of the custom textures in figure 3-34. Some were created in paint.net others were imported.

4 **Save the custom texture in the "custom textures" folder you created in Gstudio8/WAD/custom_textures as either a .TGA, .PCX, .DDS or .BMP format.**

Custom Textures figure 3-34

Info. Images imported into 3D gamestudio have to be a Power of 2 - example; 2 pixel, 4 pixel, 8 pixel etc. Images can be no larger than 1024 x 1024.

Info. Texture names must use normal letters, digits and underscore. Do not use spaces or special characters. If a texture name begins with a "+" sign followed by a digit the texture will be animated and cycle between "+0... and up to +9". If the texture name begins with "*" the texture will be a passable turbulence texture. Sky textures begin with "sky".

Adding A Custom Texture to the Textures Library

1 **Right Click on the “standard. wad” under the Textures Tab.** figure 3-35

2 **Click on ADD TEXTURE figure 3-35**

3 **In the Window that opens navigate to GStudio7/WAD/ custom_textures. figure 3-36**

4 **Open the “custom_textures” folder. figure 3-36**

5 **Select your custom texture ➔ CLICK OPEN**

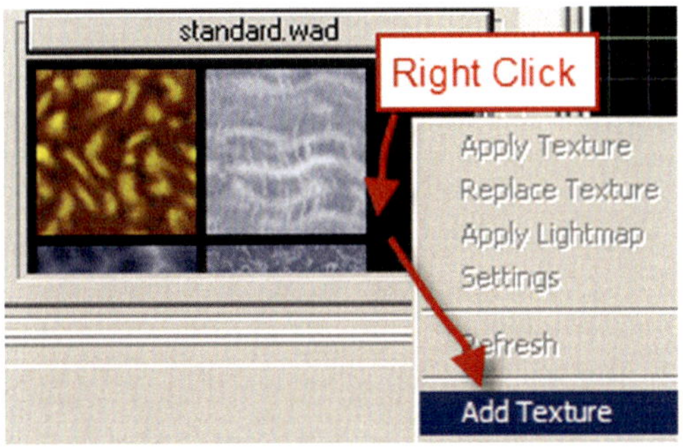

figure 3-35

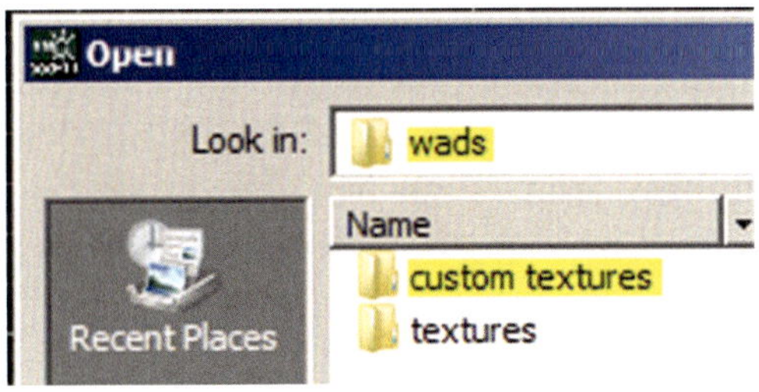

figure 3-36

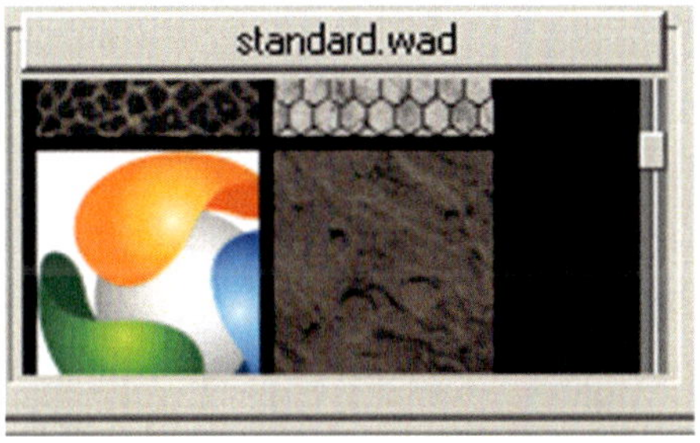

figure 3-37
Custom texture added to the custom folder and opened and ready to use.

Go to the standard.wad and scroll down to see the custom texture added to the textures.

3D Gamestudio Manual

"A texture is just a tiled image file that appears on a surface or a whole block. "
"Textures can be selected either from WAD texture collections, or from image folders on your PC. Any number of WADs or folders can be added to your map for selecting textures from them.
From Conitec Online Manual 2012

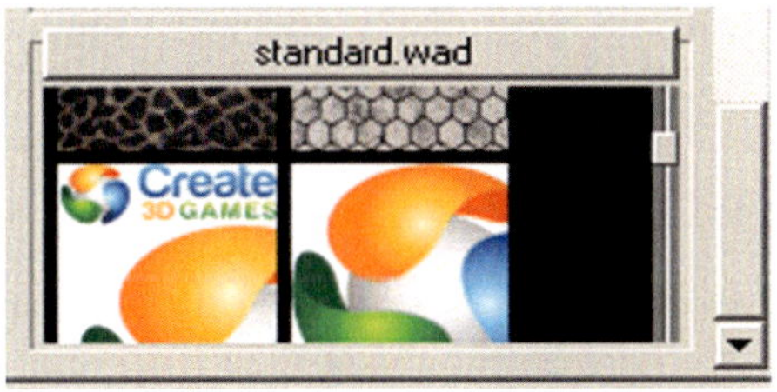

figure 3-38

Adding A Custom Texture to the Textures Library - continued

Adding a WAD

1 RIGHT CLICK on TEXTURES under the PRESETS/TEXTURES Tab.

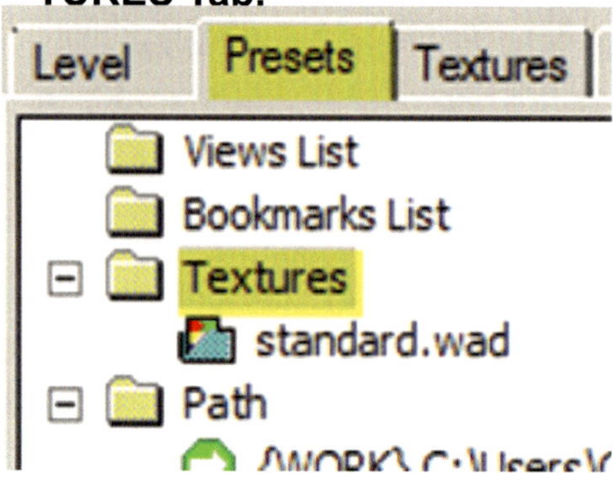

figure 3-39

2 SELECT - ADD WAD

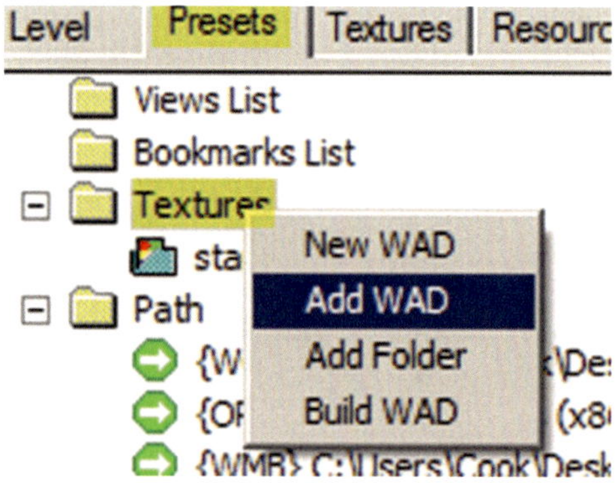

figure 3-40

Add Folder with images

1 RIGHT CLICK on TEXTURES under the PRESETS/TEXTURES Tab.

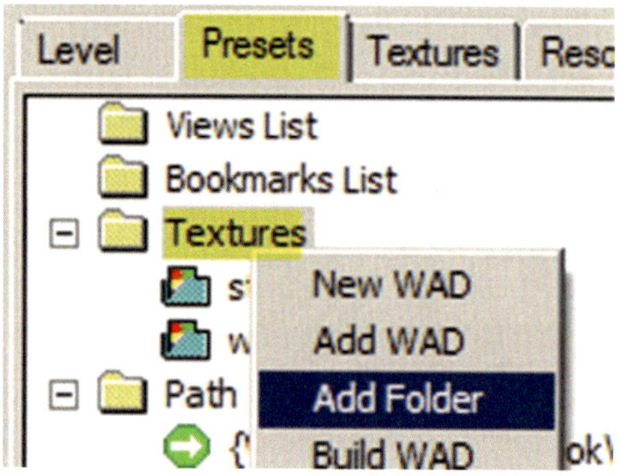

figure 3-41

2 SELECT - ADD FOLDER.

"You can import your own textures into a WAD collection. For this, first add the WAD ... and open it in the [Textures] window. Right click inside the WAD and select [Add Texture]. Then navigate to the image file that you want to add. Please note that you can't use just any image; surface textures images must fulfil some requirements." See the Online Manual - Section - Surface Textures for more information.
From Conitec Online Manual 2012
(See page 38)

New WAD

1 RIGHT CLICK on TEXTURES under the PRESETS/TEXTURES Tab.

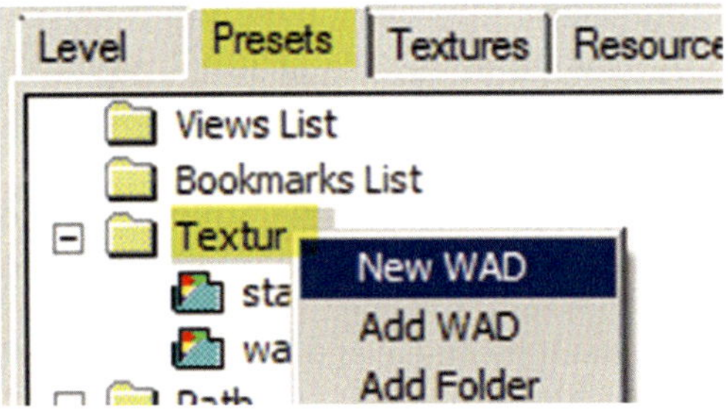

figure 3-42

2 Name the new WAD and CLICK SAVE

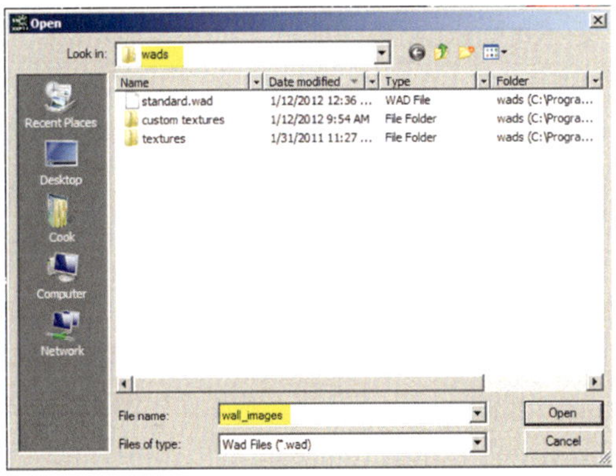

figure 3-43

There are many ways to add custom textures to 3D Gamestudio.

The example on page 39 added custom textures to the existing textures library, standard.wad.

3 Open the WAD in the Textures Window.

figure 3-44

Figure 3-39 shows the New WAD "wall_images" on the Textures Tab.

Applying the Custom Texture

1 **On the PROPERTIES TAB - under the Group named Back Room - rename the side wall "custom texture".** (Refer to page 41 for labeling Groups and Blocks)

2 **On the LEVEL TAB - Highlight the Block that has been labeled "custom texture", because that is the wall the "custom texture" of Create 3D Games logo will be applied to.**

3 **Click and highlight the inner side of the wall block.**

4 **With the "custom texture" Block highlighted ➔ GO to the SURFACE TAB and rotate through the "surfaces of the 'custom texture block" until the Inside Wall is highlighted and ready for a texture. Watch the visual display of the "current" side and check the 3D View and the other views to be sure you have highlighted the correct side of the block.**

5 **On the TEXTURE TAB either Double Click on the Custom Texture or Right Click on the Custom Texture and Click Apply**.

figure 3-45

Custom texture applied to wall.

figure 3-46

Click off the highlighted wall to see the texture.

Figure 3-47 shows the custom texture added to the standard.wad.
Figure 3-45 shows the "custom texture" wall highlighted red. The wall will be highlited red before and after applying the custom texture.
After the texture has been applied click off the highlighted wall to see the texture. figure 3-46

Adjusting Textures on the X Scale and Y Scale

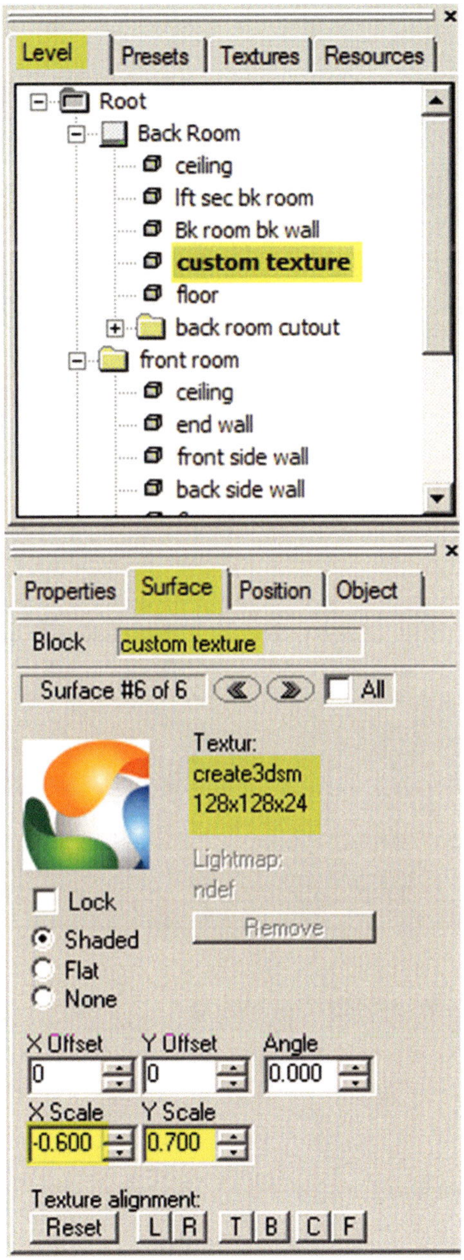

figure 3-47

Level Tab and Surface Tab after custom texture has been applied.

X and Y Scales

Use the adjustment keys on the X Scale and the Y Scale to adjust the applied texture.

A straight pattern like the Create 3D Games logo will not require any adjustments on the Angle.

The tile floor in figures 3-45, 3-46, 3-48, and 3-49 were previously scaled down. The floor is an example of an angled textured.

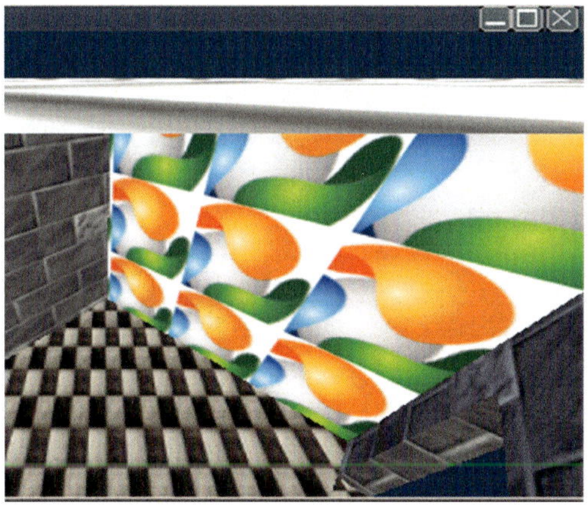

Aligning the texture. figure 3-48

Adjusting Textures on the X Scale and Y Scale

"Custom texture" adjusted on the SURFACE TAB - X Scale and the Y Scale and Offset scale to create a custom texture for the entire side wall of the second room. figure 3-49

3D Gamestudio Manual

"In the Gamestudio online store you can purchase a high resolution replacement of the standard textures, including a WAD file that contains normalmaps for all surface textures."
From Conitec Online Manual 2012

Real Time View of X and Y and Offset Adjustments

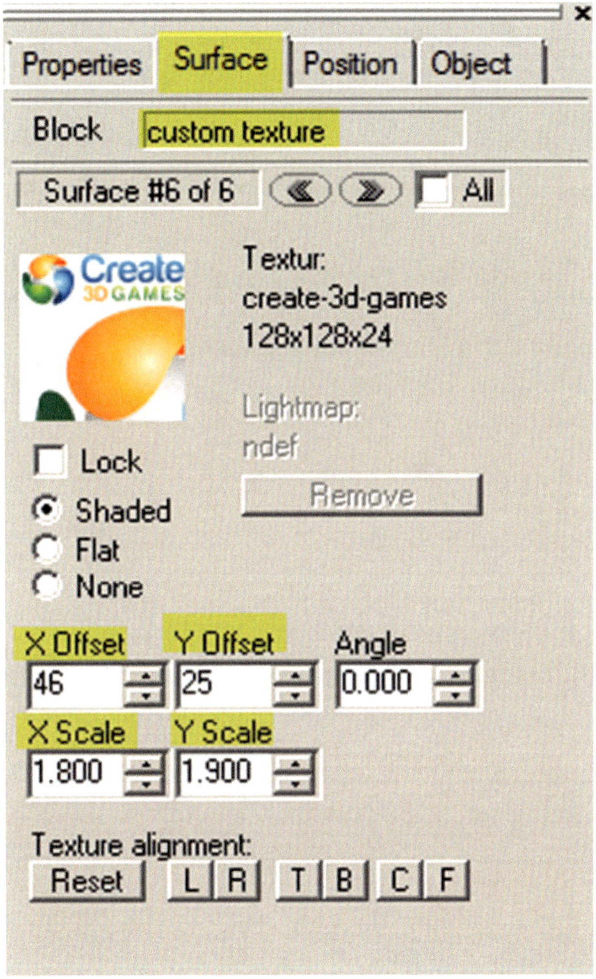

figure 3-50

1. **Zoomed into the 3D View -**
2. **Open the LEVEL TAB**
3. **Highlight the block you want to adjust**
4. **Click on the SURFACE TAB**
5. **Click through the surfaces to the surface where you want to adjust the texture.**
6. **Make adjustments and watch them change in real time in the 3D view.**

Sprites - Attaching Custom Textures to the Wall

Sprites are flat 2D objects. They can be attached to walls or floors. Use them as stand alone billboards. Use PCX, BMP, TGA or DDS files when creating the artwork in external paint programs like Paint.net or Photoshop.

1 **Click Object - Add Cube - Small.**

2 **Scale the cube down to the size of a picture on a wall, thin rectangle. figure 3-53**

3 **Line up the cube/block to the "Inside Wall" of the second room. figure 3-53**
The lines should touch. Do not hollow the Block. You could Texture the entire block the same as the wall texture it will be attached to, then the thin sides of the small block won't be noticed.

4 **With the cube/block highlighted apply your custom texture**

5 **Make adjustments on the X Scale and Y Scale.**

6 **After applying the texture to the front surface of the small cube, keep the cube surface highlighted while you make the X and Y scaling adjustments and the Offset adjustments. You can watch the changes live in the 3D view.**

figure 3-51

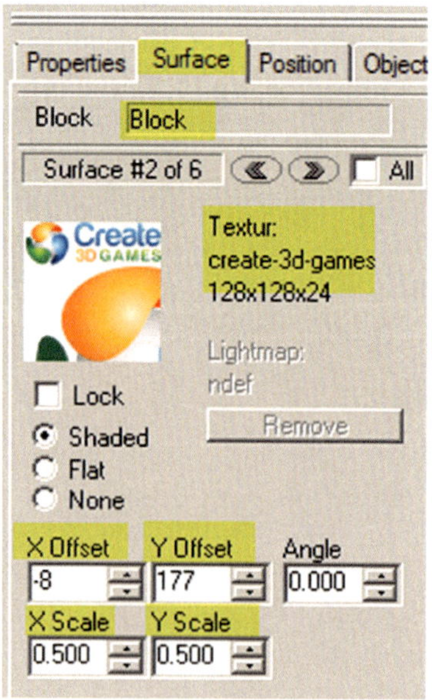

figure 3-52

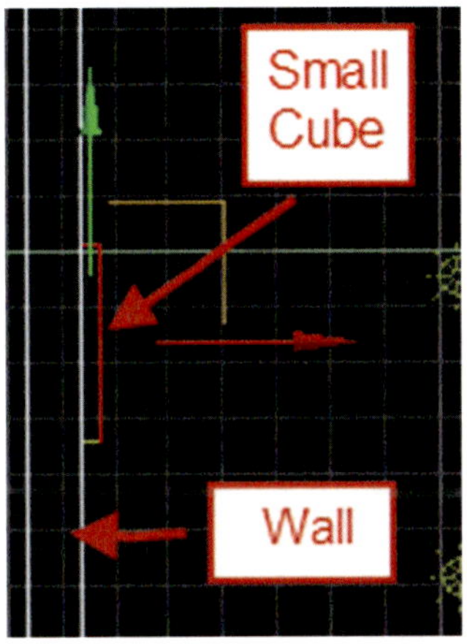

figure 3-53

This small cube is not hollowed.

The cube is simply used as a picture frame to hold the custom texture.
Scale the cube down and make it narrow (thin) to attach on the wall by lining up the back side of the small cube to the inside wall line. (Check all views to be sure the new small cube is positioned up from the floor and properly aligned to the inside wall. Zoom all the way in for precise alignment.) Place the inner wall surface against the outer back surface of the small cube. Highlight the small cube and apply the custom texture to the front side of the new small thin cube surface. (See Applying Texture page 40)

figure 3-54

Custom texture applied to small thin unhollowed cube attached to the wall. (Sprite)

Chapter 4 -
Creating a Level with Primitives

Gamestudio's Primitives

3D graphic elements are created from points, lines and triangles. 3D model files contain vertex information which includes among other things the X, Y and Z positions. A 3D object consists of 3D points, X, Y, and Z.

Primitive objects are designed in space using the Cartesian coordinate system and positions are mapped in the X, Y, and Z planes. The center of the 3D graphics world is (0, 0, 0) the **origin**. The X, Y and Z coordinates determine where in space the game objects are positioned.

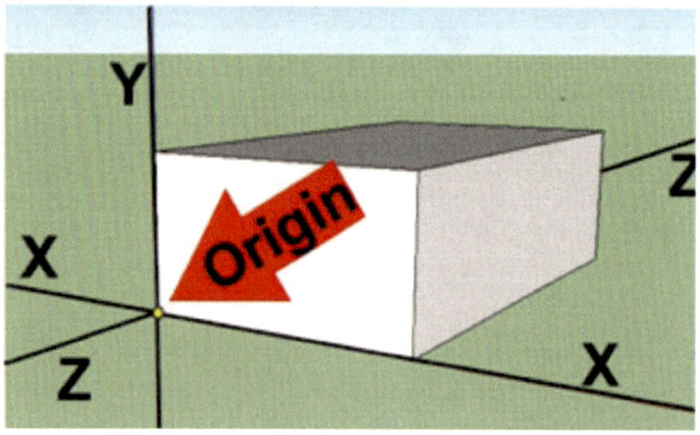

figure 4-1

The Gamestudio objects are created from Primitives. Primitives are by definition “the basic, original, or at the beginning.” There are three primary elements in the Gamestudio level; blocks, terrain and entities. **Gamestudio defines their blocks as “a solid, non-animated textured object in any shape.”**

Primitives are non-animated.
Primitives are 3-dimensional shapes.

Primitives can be textured the same as cubes. They have different surface sides that appear on the Surfaces Tab.

The Gamestudio software has an extensive list of **Pre-Fabs** on the menu bar under OBJECT such as; arches, bridges, buildings, furniture, etc. Users have the option of importing primitives from outside 3D libraries. See the Help Menu within Gamestudio's software for information about importing files.

OBJECT ➔ ADD PRIMITIVE.

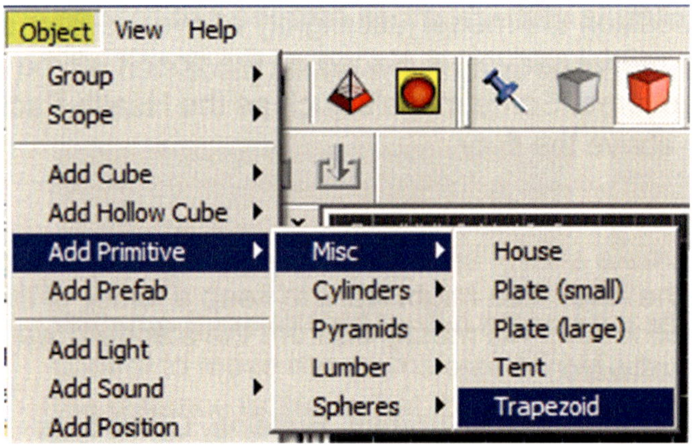

Gamestudio Primitives figure 4-2

Gamestudio primitives are computer graphic elements which are used as building blocks.

The basic concept of Gamestudio's design is the use of Object Oriented editing. Users design and create using Gamestudio's primary elements. Users piece together simple forms to create more complex forms.

Gamestudio provides several **primitives.** At the time this book was written they were; Cylinders, Pyramids, Lumber, Spheres and a miscellaneous group of primitives; House, Plate (small), Plate (large), Tent and Trapezoid.

These primitives are found under **Object ➔ Add Primitives.**

Aligning Rooms continued

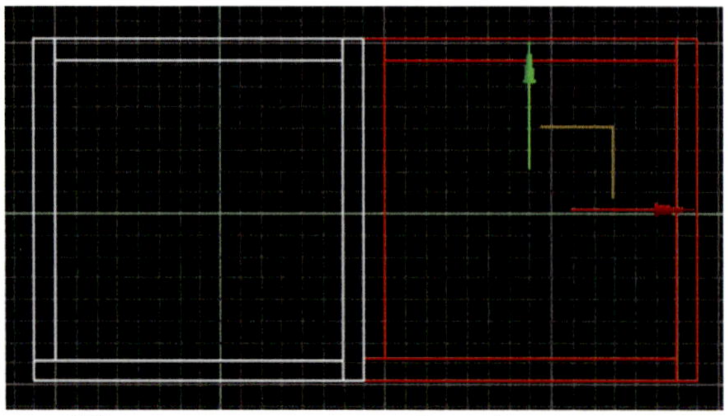

figure 4-7

The rooms are overlapping.

IMPORTANT Blocks that are aligned to each other and have good verticle and horizontal edges in all three views compile and render faster!

So before you start aligning rooms - be sure to ALIGN TO GRID the very first room (group) Then after that be sure to align all the objects and have the rooms aligned perfectly and the objects aligned to the grid. If you need to change the grid and make it more precise the grid can be changed in the Preference menu, view option.

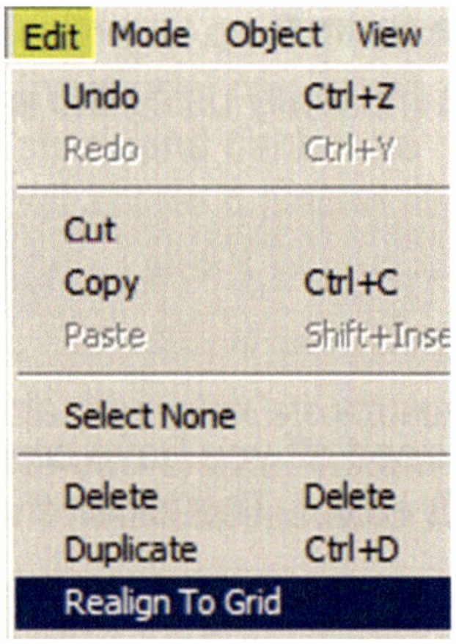

Realign to Grid figure 4-8

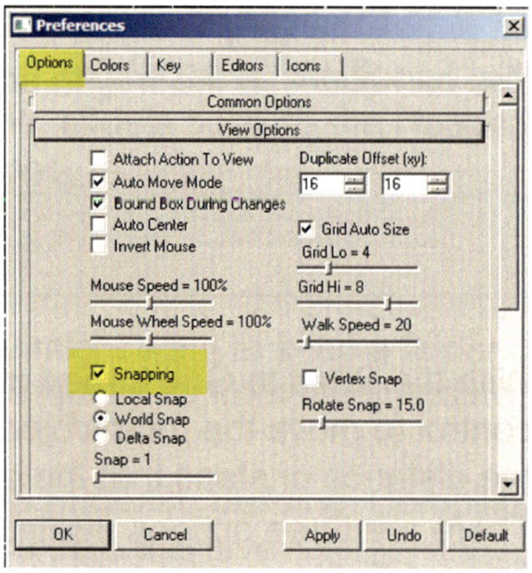

Preferences figure 4-9

Aligning and Snapping

Click File ➔ Preference and open the View Options. Check Snapping.
Set the scale at 1 or 2 - the rooms will overlap and align easily. In Chapter 2 snapping was set, be sure that snapping is still set. figure 4-5
GO TO CENTER - often when working with large rooms, zooming in and out will place the images in the four windows out of your view.
Click on View - GO TO CENTER, or HOME to center all the views.

8 **ALIGN ALL THE ROOMS** (outside lines overlapped) figure 4-12 (Holes will be cut (CSG Subtract) between the front room and the back room and a hole will be cut in the ceiling of the back room.

9 **TEXTURE THE ROOMS** - texture an entire group - or - texture each side (block) by switching back and forth between the Level Tab and the Textures Tab - highlighting the individual sides (blocks) then click on the Textures Tab and the Surface Tab to apply a texture to the individual side highlighted under the Levels Tab. figure 4-10, figure 4-11 (Refer to Chapter 3)

10 **CREATE WALL IMAGES (Sprites)** by adding an unhollowed cube and scaling it like a picture frame and adhering a texture to the unhollowed cube. figure 4-13, Refer to pages 58-59.

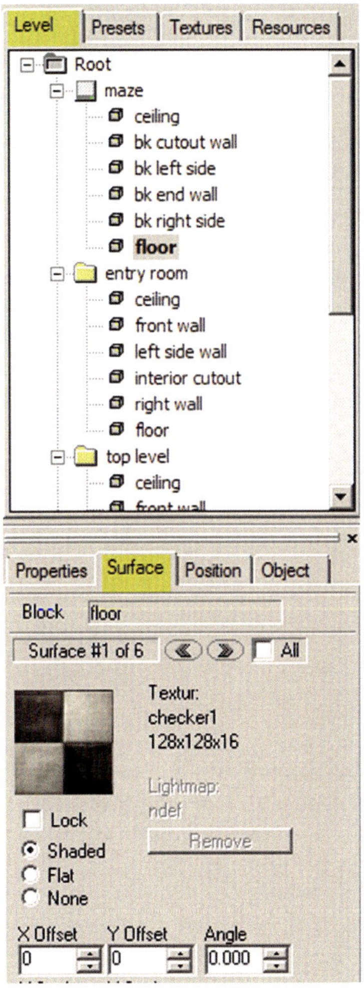

figure 4-10

Levels Tab/Surface Tab

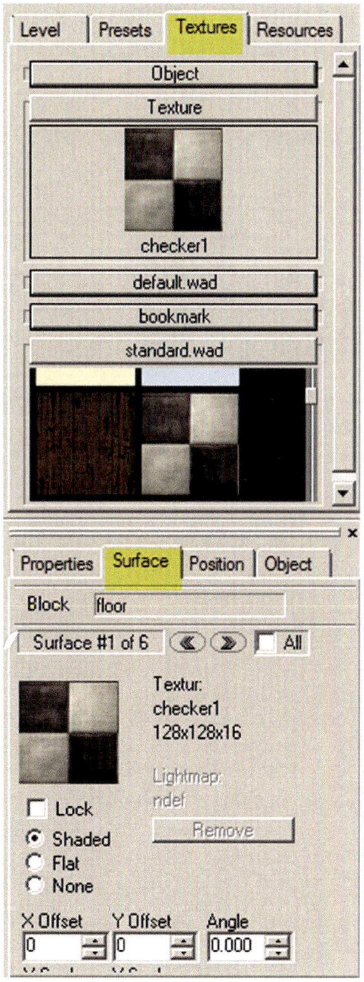

figure 4-11

Texture Tab/Surface Tab

11 **MATCH THE FLOOR TEXTURE PATTERNS.** pages 36-40

12 **LABEL THE BLOCKS** - front room, back wall etc. page 37

13 **ADD LIGHTS TO THE ROOMS (Object ➔ Add Lights) Increase and decrease light intensity using the arrow keys while on the Level Tab.**

14 **ADD A POSITION in the front room** (Object ➔Add Position,camera)

15 **Click File ➔ Save**

16 **Click on BUILD THE LEVEL**  **- Click OK on MAP COMPILER ➔ Click OK to close compiler.**

17 **Click on RUN -**  **use the arrow keys to zoom into the compiled level and check your work. Move the camera position around with the mouse.**

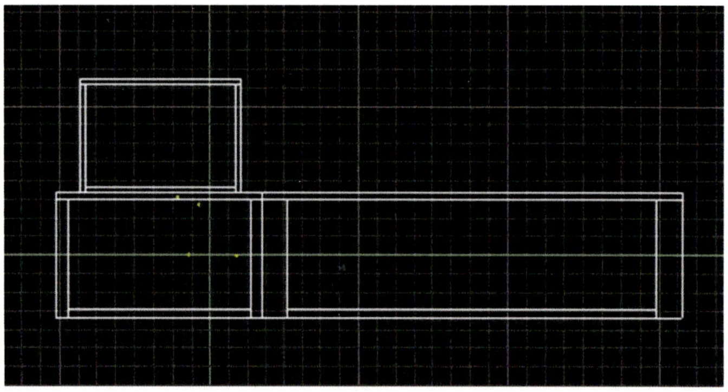

Three rooms aligned.

figure 4-12

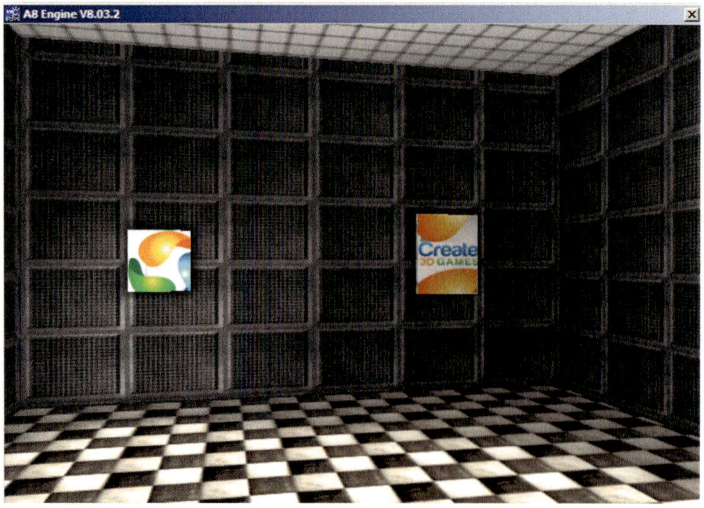

Front Room with sprites (pictures) on the wall.

figure 4-13

18 Click Object ➔ Add Cube ➔Large

19 POSITION the large cube between the two bottom rooms and CSG SUBTRACT AN OPENING between the rooms. (CSG SUBTRACT refer to pages 25, 26, 27)

20 Click Object ➔Add Cube ➔ Large

21 POSITION the large cube between the top room and the back bottom room. CSG SUBTRACT AN OPENING BETWEEN THE ROOMS.

22 Click File ➔ Save

23 Click on BUILD THE LEVEL ➔ Click OK on Map Compiler ➔ Click OK to close compiler.

24 Click on RUN use the arrow keys to zoom into the compiled level and check your work. Move the camera position around with the mouse.

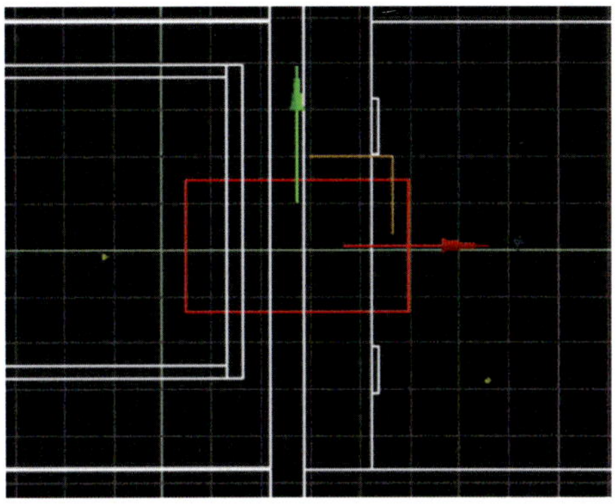

Figure 4-14 shows the large block positioned between the front and back rooms.

Figure 4-15 shows the finished CSG Subtract with the cutout walls textured and the floor in the cutout textured.

figure 4-14

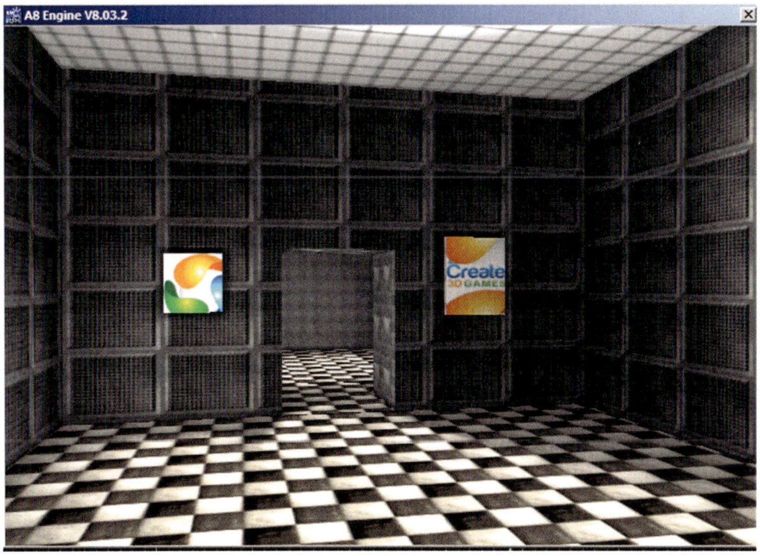

Info.
Save the level often.
Build and run the level often and check your work.

figure 4-15

The two bottom rooms will be filled with primitives. The front room will be a maze. The first primitive to be placed in the room will be the a piece of lumber, which will be the barriers for the maze.

25 Object ➔Add Primitive ➔ Lumber ➔ 8x8
Scale the Lumber into long panels

26 With the piece of lumber highlighted Click on texture and texture the entire piece of lumber.

27 SCALE THE TEXTURE (This texture has a black and yellow pattern which was brought to the top of barrier.

28 Right Click on the barrier and duplicate the barrier several times. Or, hold down the control key and hit D.

29 Fill the front room with barriers placed in a maze pattern.

30 Click Object ➔ Add Primitive ➔ Plate and texture the plate and place it on top of the first two barriers.

31 Click Object ➔ Add Primitive ➔ Cylinder

32 With the cylinder highlighted Click on EDIT BOX and size the cylinder and ROTATE and flip the cylinder onto its side.

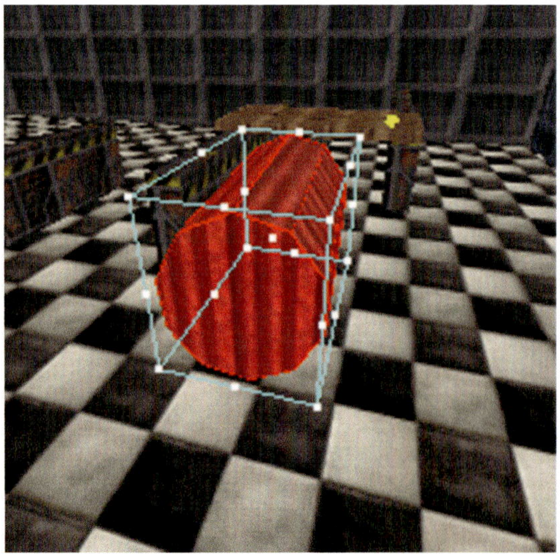

The cylinder is by default solid. This cyclinder will be hollowed using the CSG Subtract.

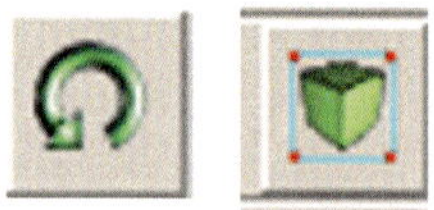

Cylinder flipped on side using the Rotate button and sized using the Edit Box.

figure 4-16

34 Position the cylinder under the Plate

35 Click File ➔ Save

36 Click on build the level ➔ Click on Map Compiler ➔ Click OK to close the compiler

37 Click Run

figure 4-17

Grouping Objects

A Sphere (a simple primitive) and a Trapezoid (a simple primitive) have been added and have been **GROUPED** together creating a complex structure. figures 4-18, 4-19

38 With the Trapazoid highlighted Click Object ➔ GROUP ➔ G (when first added) GROUP TOGETHER and Click on the sphere, they will be grouped.

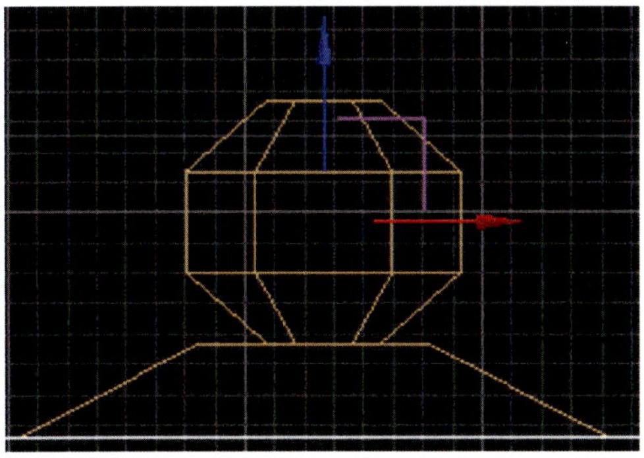

figure 4-18

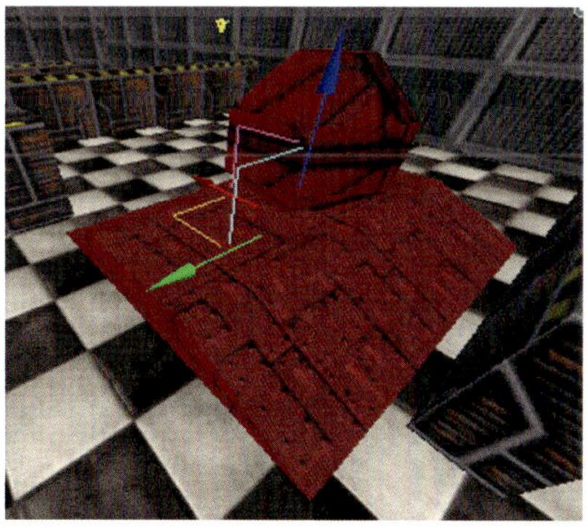

figure 4-19

When highlighted, the grouped sphere and trapezoid both turn red and are one object.

Grouping Objects - continued

With grouping and scoping, you can manipulate multiple blocks or other objects as a single object.
Add To - Adds the selected object to a group. It changes the selected object's color to orange to show that you have marked it for grouping.
Group Together - Groups the current selected objects together into a new group.
Ungroup - This command ungroups the selected group and separates its parts into individual objects.

Editing a Pre-Fab (Editing a Primitive)

As primitives are added and then textured use Scope Down to isolate the object for texturing. Highlight the object and Scope Down.

Each object will have multiple sides to texture. The texture on the Pre-Fabs can be changed. This example will change the texture on the Pre-Fab staircase "WINDIN02.WMP". There will be a hole cut in the ceiling of the back room (SCG Subtract) and the stairs will be placed through the opening.
There will also be a pool of liquid placed under the stairs with an obstacle placed in the water.

39 Click Object ➔ Add Pre-Fab ➔ Open the Pre-Fabs figure 4-20

40 Scroll down to the upstairs folder and Click on WINDIN02.WMP.
figure 4-21

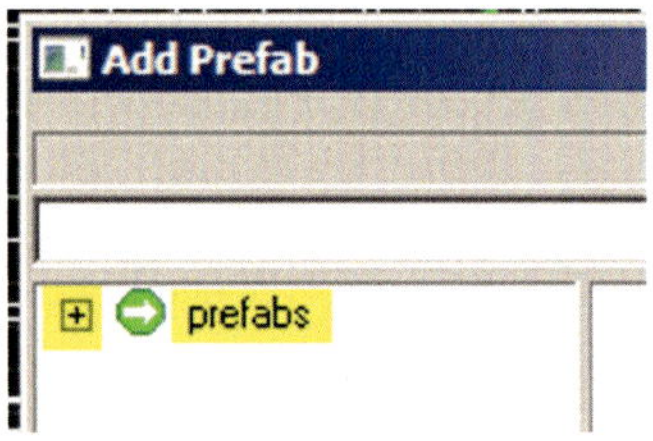

figure 4-20

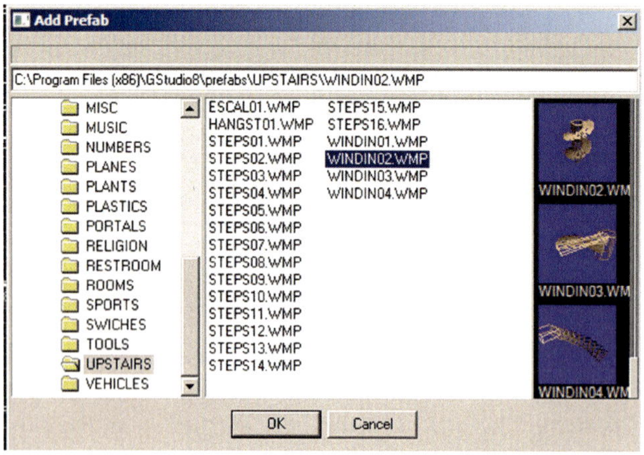

figure 4-21

PreFab WINDIN02 figure 4-22

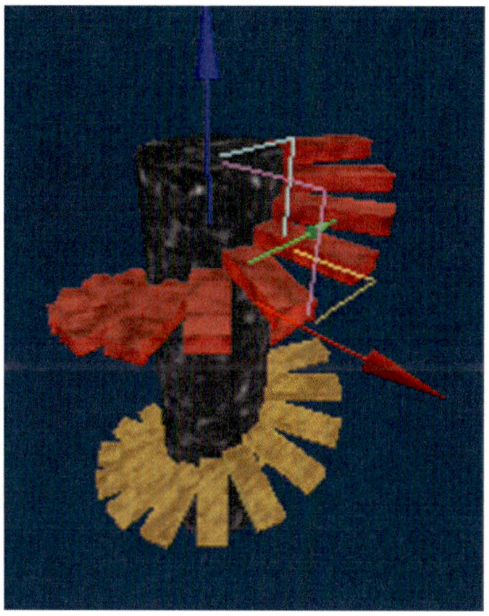

Texture Applied figure 4-23

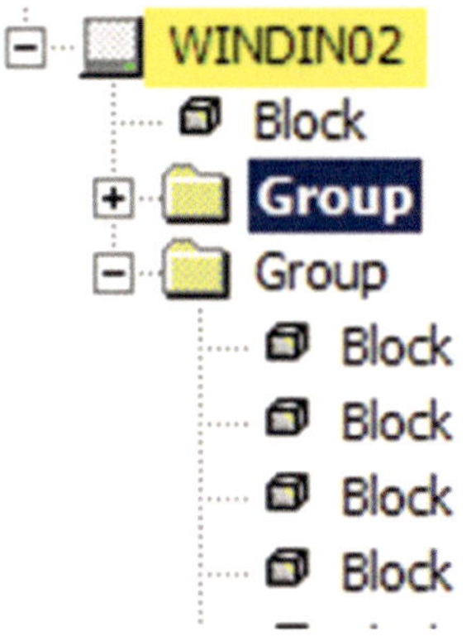

figure 4-24

Levels Tab - First Group Folder under WINDIN02 - upper portion of stairs

36 **Click on the LEVELS TAB ➔ Click on WINDIN02 FOLDER ➔ Click on the FIRST GROUP.** This will highlight the top portion of the steps. This process will texture all sides of the steps with the same texture. Opening the Group Folder will allow texturing each step separately. This example is texturing all the steps the same. figure 4-23

41 **Click on the TEXTURES TAB ➔ in the standard.wad folder choose a different color for the steps on the spiral stairway ➔ RIGHT CLICK ➔ APPLY** This example is applying a wooden texture to the steps. (woodflvert) figure 4-23

42 **REPEAT for the second group folder (**lower stairs)

43 **File ➔ Save .wmp file extension**

Leave the stairs in the back lower room. Next we'll create a CSG Subtract block and move the stairs and the CSG block around in all three views to get the precise position for the CSG ceiling cutout.

Editing a Pre-Fab - Ungrouping

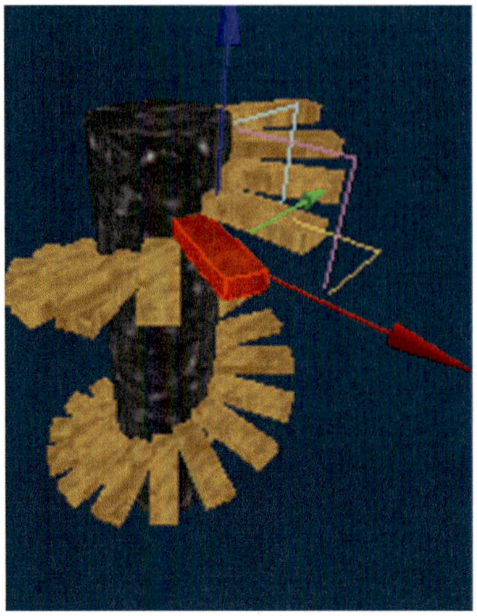

Ungrouped Pre-Fab figure 4-25

Pre-Fabs can be ungrouped. Figure 4-22 shows the upper stairs ungrouped. A few of the steps could be deleted to make the level more dangerous for the player.
To make the level more detailed the individual sides of the steps could be textured to make the steps more realistic.
Highlight the group Click Object - Group - Ungroup.

Adding an Upper Level, Adding Stairs & Scenery

44 Click Object ➔ Add Cube ➔ Large

45 Scale the Block 

46 Position the block between the top room's floor and the bottom back room's ceiling.

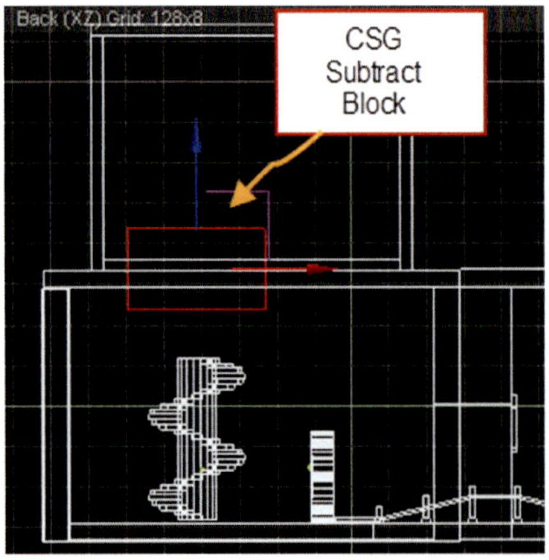

figure 4-26

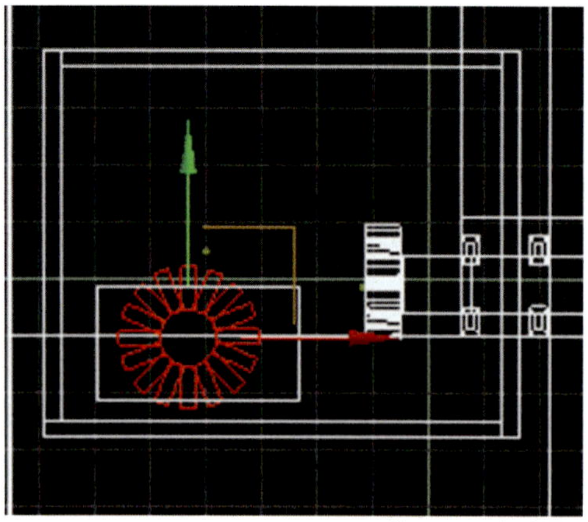

figure 4-27

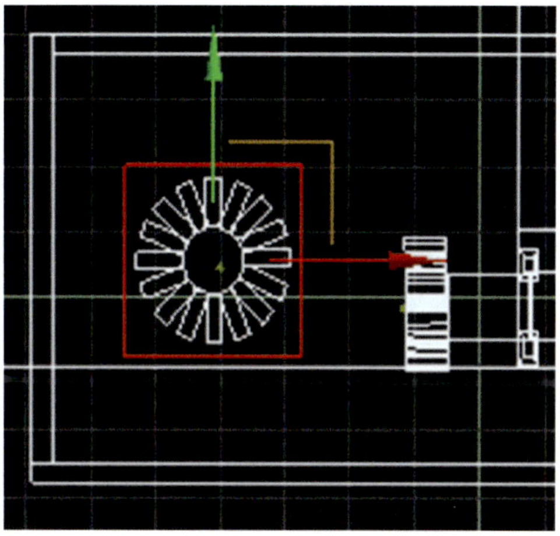

figure 4-28

Position the CSG Block in all three windows. Make sure the stairs will fit inside the cutout in all views.

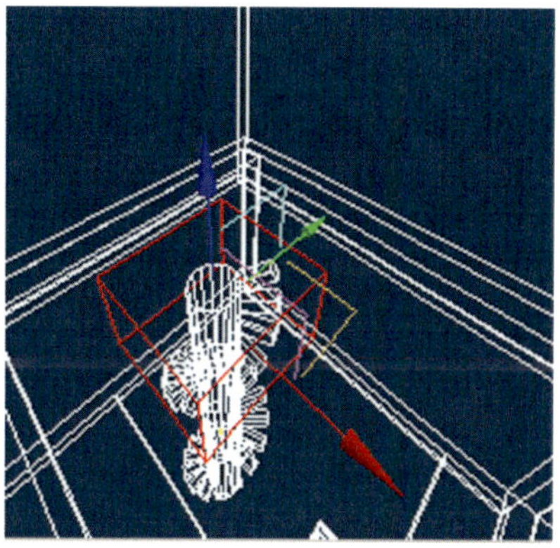

figure 4-29

VIEW ➔ WIRE FRAME
shows the CSG Subtract block in the 3D View.

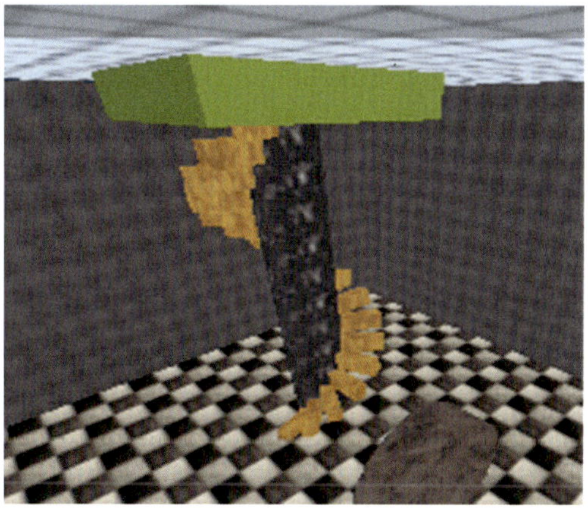

figure 4-30

Textured 3D view shows the staircase in the CSG Block.

Info. Control Z = undo

Insert Button - adds cubes, primitives, etc from the Object Menu.

47 MOVE THE STAIRS TO THE SIDE
keep the stairs are out of the CSG Subtract! ! !

48 Edit ➔CSG Subtract. (Chapter 2 pages 25, 26, 27)

49 Delete the Block used to create the CSG Subtract.

50 Texture the cutout area in the ceiling. Chapter 3 pages 34-39

51 Move the Stairs back in position under the CSG Subtract opening.

52 Save

53 Build ➔ Run

Adding Scenery

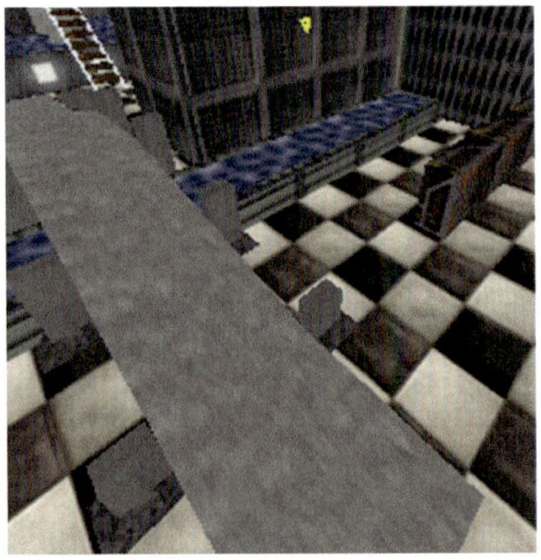

figure 4-31
Pool built from cubes placed under the ramp leading to the back room.

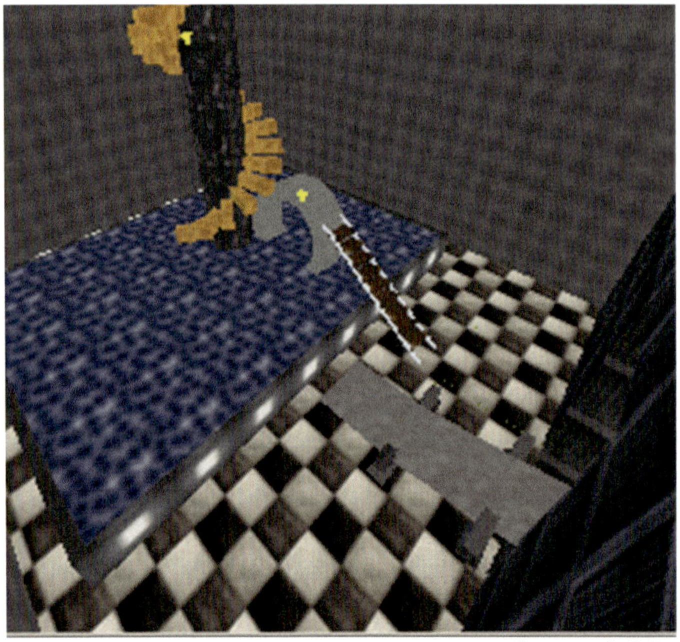

figure 4-32
Pre-Fab pool added under the staircase.

Figure 4-32 shows a pool from the Pre-Fabs library. Another way to add a pool is to create a hollowed cube. Create a BLOCK that fits down into the hollowed cube but is tall enough to remove the top portion of this hollowed cube.. CSG Subtract the Hollowed Cube. Use the CSG Subtract BLOCK as the water in the pool by now hollowing that BLOCK (which now becomes a cube). Texture the water cube with one of the water textures. Place the water cube down into the pool cube. These examples are purely scenery the pools are not at this point functioning, passable, and transparent pools of water. Players who enter the pools will walk on the surface. An easier method is to just texture the top section of a cube with the water texture when creating scenery. Many of the pre-fabs and primitives can be hollowed to create interesting scenery.

Info.

Creating a Pool that's Passable

Refer to Appendix D for a more detailed explanation of how to create a functioning pool a player can enter and swim through.

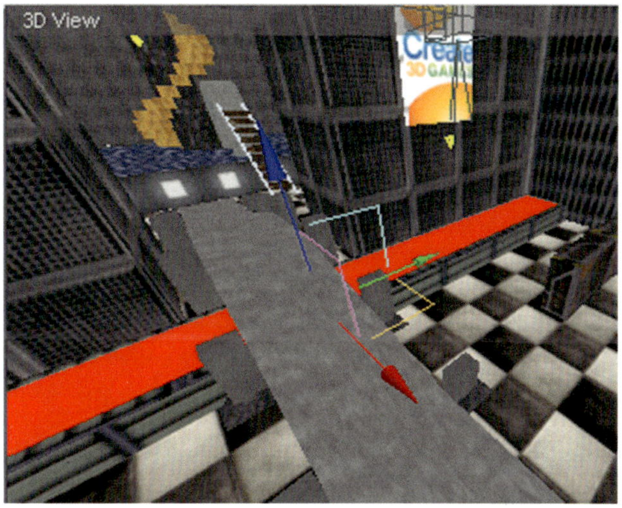

Block for CSG Subtract.

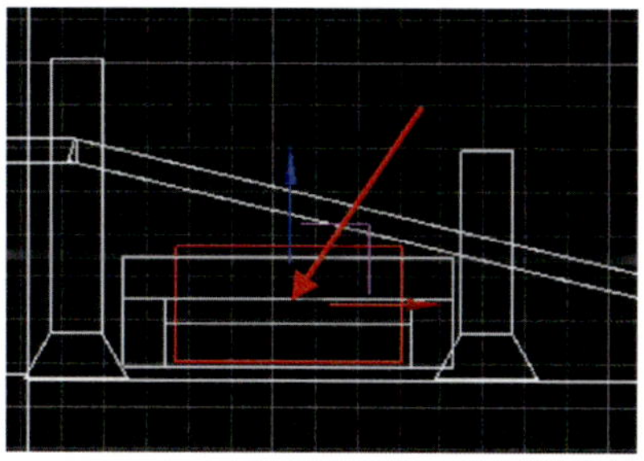

figure 4-34

figure 4-33

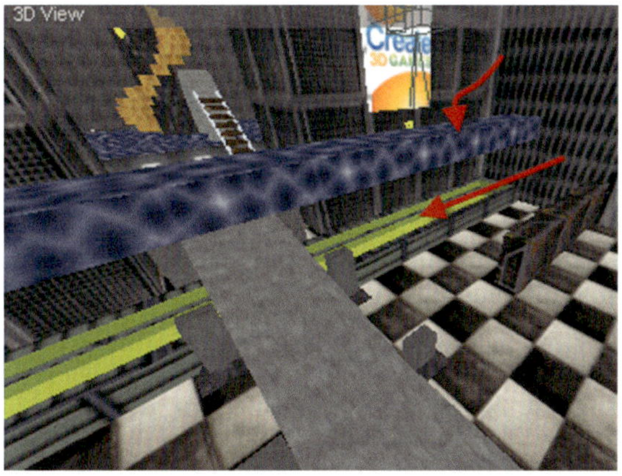

CSG Block hollowed and textured with the water cube ready to be positioned down into the pool cube.

There are many creative ways to use SCG Subtract to create an interesting environment.

figure 4-35

Created Level from players point of view inside the game.

figure 4-36

Chapter 5 - **Entities**

Gamestudio's engine supports the following ENTITIES; Models, Sprites, Sublevels (Map Entities) **and Terrain** (Unchunked and Chunked).

Entities can be created with script, or in WED. They are external files read from the path or work folder.

MODELS are animated 3D objects. They are stored in an external MDL file. Models have a 3D mesh with skeleton bones and skin. They are used as moveable or animated objects and they can cast dynamic shadows. Models are WMBs in Gamestudio's Map Entity extension.

SPRITES (Billboards) are flat 2D objects. They are stored in external PCX, BMP, TGA & DDS files, and they can be created in paint programs such as; Paint.net, Photoshop, etc. Sprites can contain an alpha channel which has a transparency value for the pixels. Earlier in this book the Arrow texture in the textures section was created and saved as a .TGA file using the Paint.net software. It was a sprite. Sprites act as Decals, they can be placed on floors or walls and they stand upright in landscapes like a billboard. If a sprite's angles are zero it stands upright and will horizontally face the camera. Four sprites can be placed as an "X" shape and create plants or trees. Set the Pan and Tilt at "0" and the roll angle at nonzero the sprite will face the camera in two directions. Animated sprites use PCS, BMP and TGA formats, the DDS format will not support animation. Refer to Chapter 3, page 46 on how to create a Sprite.

SUBLEVELS (Map Entities) are small compiled levels stored in an external .WMP file format. **They are compiled maps and can be used in the levels as moving doors, platforms, or vehicles.** They can be created in WED. PreFabs can be converted into Map Entities by loading the PreFab as a Map and Building the Map Entity then copying it as a .WMB file and placing it in the current level directory.

TERRAIN is one or more textures mapped onto a rectangular grid of height values. They can be created with MED, imported from RAW height maps, or can be built with terrain builder programs and imported BMP, PCX height image bitmaps. Passable terrains such as water allow characters in a game to wade, swim or dive. The engine supports unchunked and chunked terrain. Chunked terrain allows faster terrain rendering.

Downloading Models from Gamestudio's website

Version 8 of Conitec's Gamestudio does not have models in the WED. Models are available at Conitec's website. The following instructions are for downloading the Gamestudio 8 models, if you have a paid version of the software.

IMPORTANT - This Chapter will explain downloading the levels8.zip file that contains the model entities. The next chapter "Creating a Game" will show how and when to add the models into the level. This chapter may seem out of sequence but if we download the models now we can flow right into adding the models in the next chapter without stopping to add the models.

DO THIS NOW!

Go to http://www.gamestudio.com

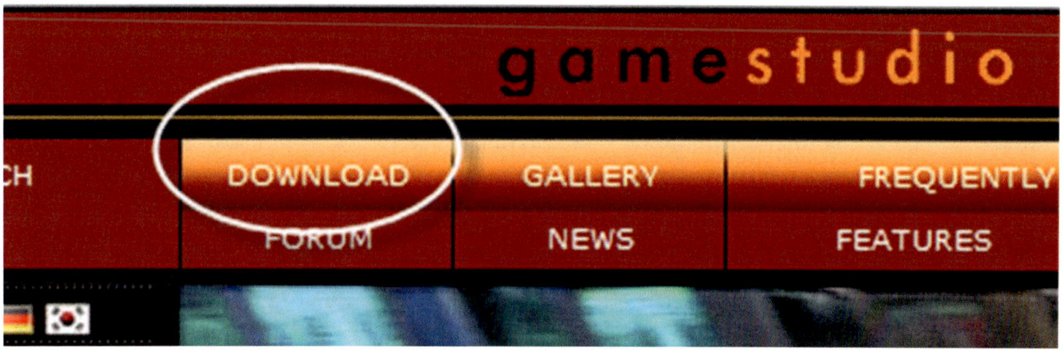

figure 5-1

1 Click download on the Conitec Gamestudio website. figure 5-1

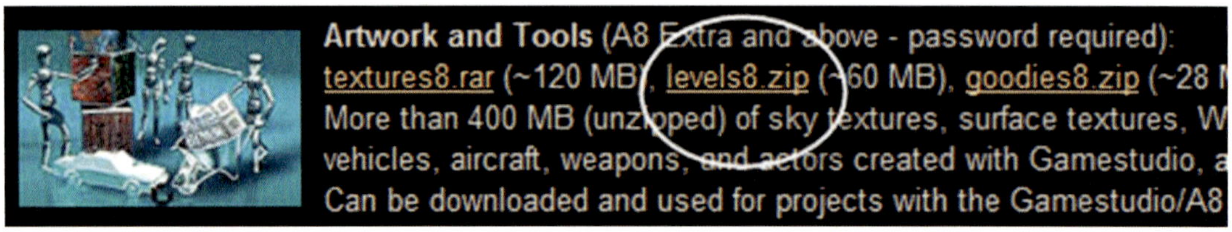

figure 5-2

2 Download the "levels8.zip" file from Conitec's website. figure 5-2

3 Enter the User Name and Password for the Gamestudio Software you purchased. figure 5-3

figure 5-3

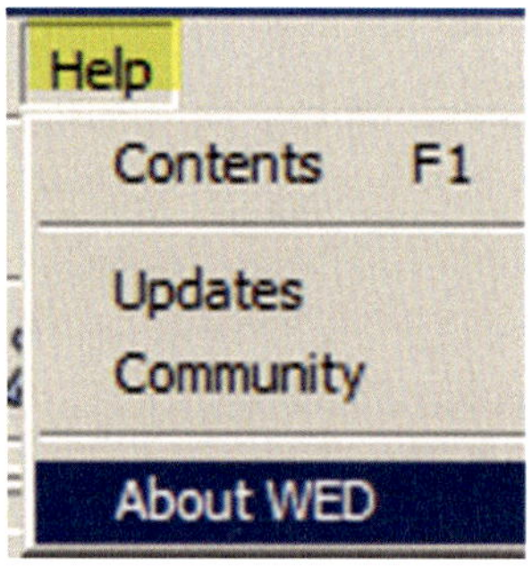

figure 5-4

FIND YOUR USER NAME – PASSWORD by looking in the WED, Click on HELP ➔ Click on About WED.

4 Save the levels8.zip file in your Work folder.
The "Models" (players) are found in the levels8.zip file.

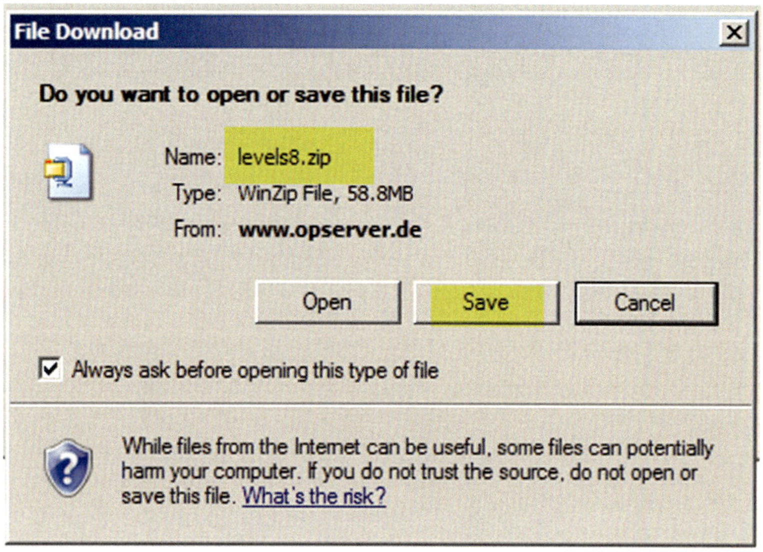

figure 5-5

5 **Place the unzipped levels8 folder containing the model files into the directory where 3D GameStudio was installed. (C:\Program Files\ GStudio8 (The downloaded files should be saved in the work folder)**

Within Gamestudio WED check the Presets tab to see where the folders/ files have been placed. Correct placement of the download is important to be able to open the files and load them into Gamestudio.

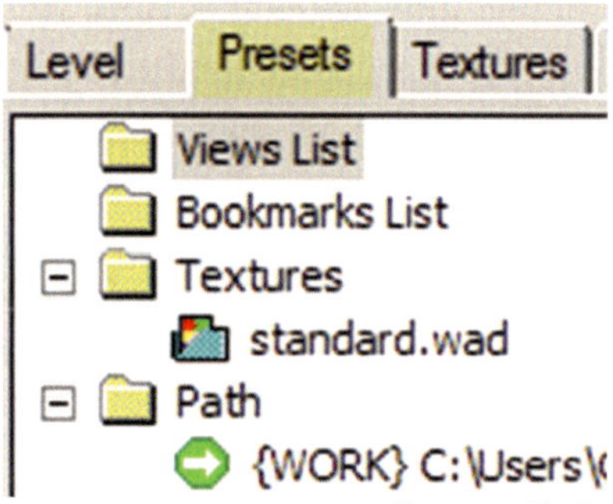

figure 5-6

6 **UNZIP the levels8 file in the work folder.**

Chapter 6 - **Creating a Game**

CREATE A GAME
FIRST - Create your level
SECOND - Add a Template Script

Map Properties - Adding a Script

A script is required for the first level of a game. To program a game yourself use "Empty Script." This example will use a Gamestudio **game genre** which uses a predefined template script.
A **Script** is either a program or a sequence of instructions another program interprets and runs. **Template scripts** have functions and artwork used for the interface, effects, player movement, enemies etc. These templates allow users to create games without requiring any programming.
All of the template scripts can be combined and customized for various games. New scripts are available at Gamestudio's website in the template section of the user forum and in the magazine AUM. figure 6-1

New scripts can be created using the Lite-C program. Lite -C is based off of C++ and will require programming knowledge. Conitec provides tutorials that teach the basics of the Lite-C program. Information about Lite-C will be touched on in the Appendix.

This example will cover; opening a level, using the Map Properties, Property Manager, Load Entities (players), and Assigning Behavior "Actions" to the players in a game using a template script. This book is using the Gamestudio / Atari lite-C Version 8.31.

ACKNEX Users Magazine

http://www.3dgamestudio.com/ figure 6-1

The AUM magazine is published online monthly at the gamestudio website. It is for Gamestudio users. It contains workshops about programming for gamestudio software, tips, tricks , news and other information. It is edited by George Pirvu. The shooter game template script provided by Conitec under the template scripts was written by George Pirvu.

1 **Design and Create a Level for your game.**
This book's example has two bottom rooms; a front room with a maze and small pool of water and a back room with a larger pool of water with a staircase leading to the upper level room. This book's level is named primitive_demo.wmp.This chapter will assume the user has a level created, textured and open.

2 **Click on File ➔ SAVE AS**
IMPORTANT - you must File-Save As before a script is added.
(Not Save but SAVE AS)
(name your Level without using spaces in the name, this book's example is named primitive_demo.wmp)

3 **The next step is to ADD a SCRIPT.** This example is using a template script provided by Conitec.

4 **In the WED ➔ Click on File ➔Build Map ➔ Click "OK"** Figures 6-2,, 6-3, 6-4

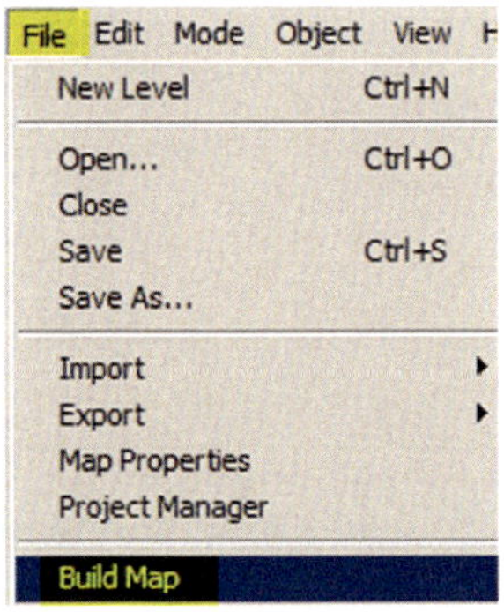

Build Map

Build converts the map into the .wmb file format.

figure 6-2

Info. When creating levels users should SAVE the level often, BUILD the level often, and RUN the level to check their work. With a level created, saved and error free the next step is to add a script.

Map Properties - Adding a Script continued

Building the Map.

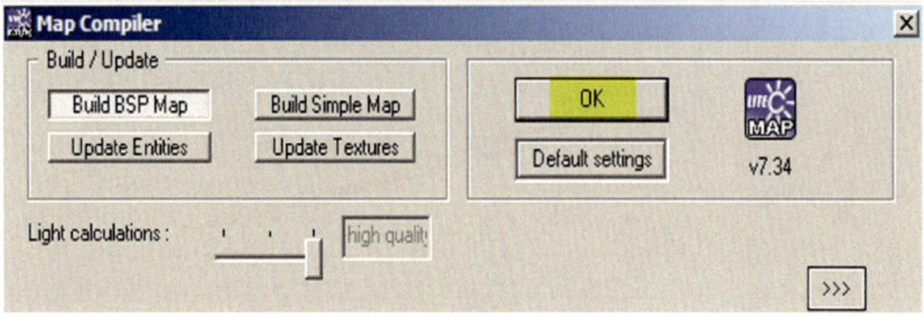

Map Compiler

figure 6-3

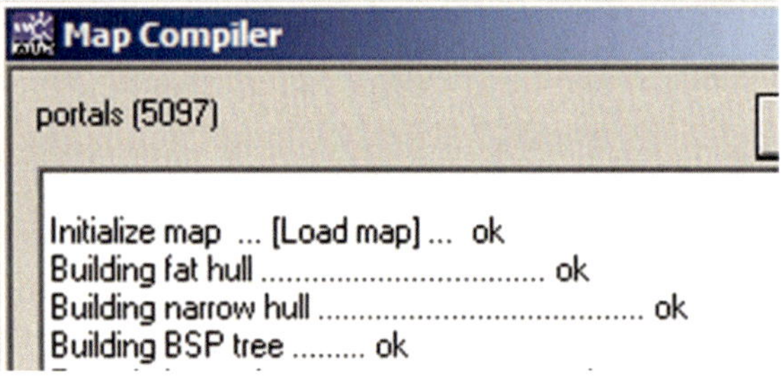

Compiling

figure 6-4

5 Click File ➔ Map Properties ➔ Click on the Folder beside Palette
Figures 6-6, (select the file you want to build your game in. (Our example is primitive_demo.wmp)

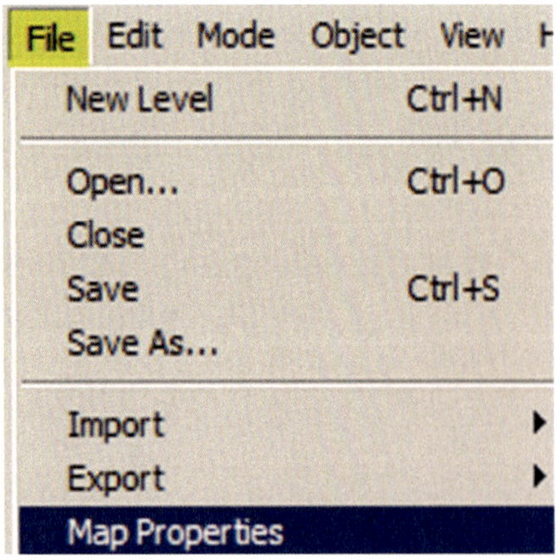

Map Properties

figure 6-5

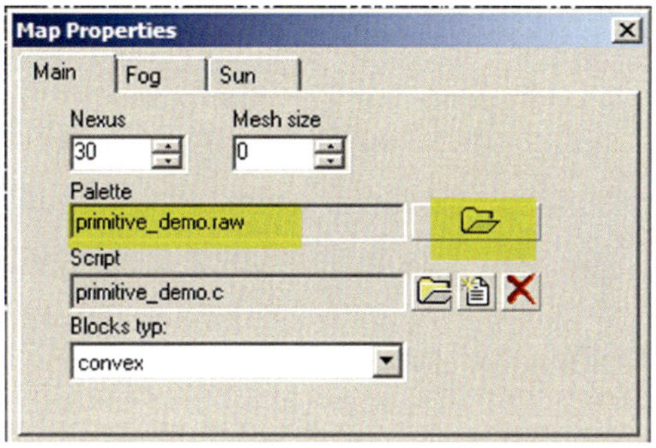

figure 6-6

6 **Click on the file beside File Name ➔ Click Open.** Under the **Work Folder** choose the file you are working on. (Ours is primitive_demo.wmp) **The file loads into the Palette.** figure 6-6

7 **Next, Click on the NEW SCRIPT ICON next to Script.** figure 6-7 The "Which script do you want to create?" menu opens. figure 6-8

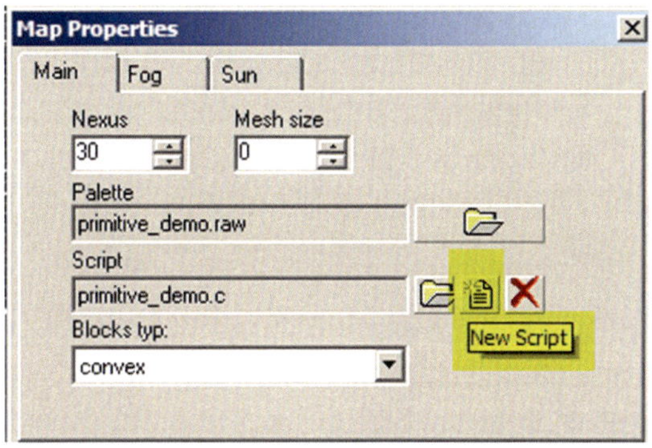

Map Properties: figure 6-7
Script:
The folder icon is the Open Scripts.
The page icon is the New Script
The name under "Script" is the Script Level with the .c script file.
To delete the script click on the red X.
figure 6-7

8 **With the window "Which Script do you want to Create" open Check the Template Projecton ➔ Click OK.** figure 6-8 This creates the .c file in the Map Properties Script panel.

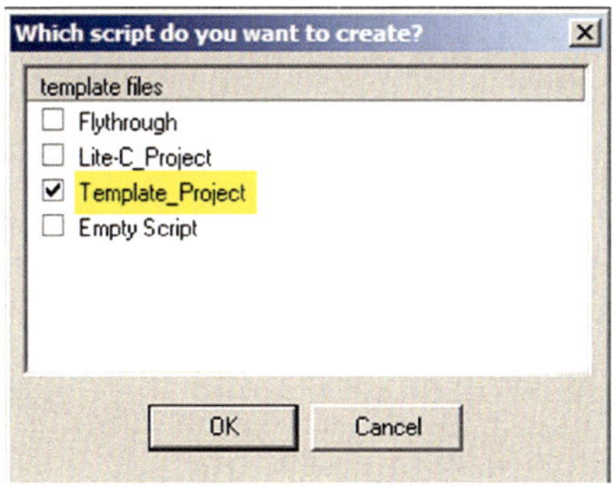

figure 6-8

At the time this book was published these were the script options Conitec provided in the Map Properties New Script Folder. figure 6-8
Conitec changes this list with the different versions. Earlier software versions had more template scripts. Users of the software now write most of their own scripts using Conitec's SED, Script Editor.

Map Properties - Adding a Script

Script Options:

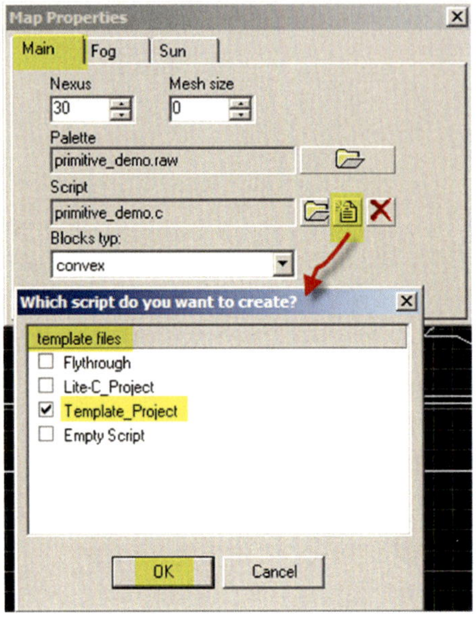

figure 6-9

The scripts provided by Conitec at the time this book was written were:

Flythrough - Loads the current map as a level. It allows the user/player to fly through the level using the cursor keys.
Lite-C_Project - this loads the current map as a level. It includes the standard shaders. The rest of the project creation is up to the user.
Template_Project - Creates a main script. This is the selection this book will be using. Check Template Project and click OK. Then open the Project Manager to add the individual script templates.
Empty Script - This creates a script and does not contain anything else. The creation of the script is up to the user.

Prior to 2007 the gamestudio programming software was coded in C-Script. The Map Properties Script used was a .wdl file. **Today Conitec's gamestudio uses Lite-C and creates a .c script file.**

http://www.opserver.de/ubb7/

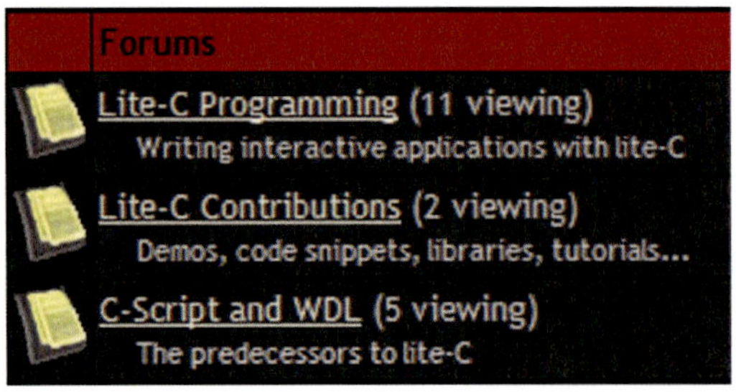

figure 6-10

When using an Empty Script users create their own code with the Lite-C software in gamestudio's SED, Script Editor. Users can find code in the forums on gamestudio's website and from the AUM magazine.
Some of the code online will be in the older .wdl format which requires modifications depending on the version of Gamestudio you are using.

THIRD - next step in creating a game - open the Project Manager

Project Manager - adding game scripts

1 **In the WED ➔ Click on File ➔ Click on Project Manager.** figure 6-11

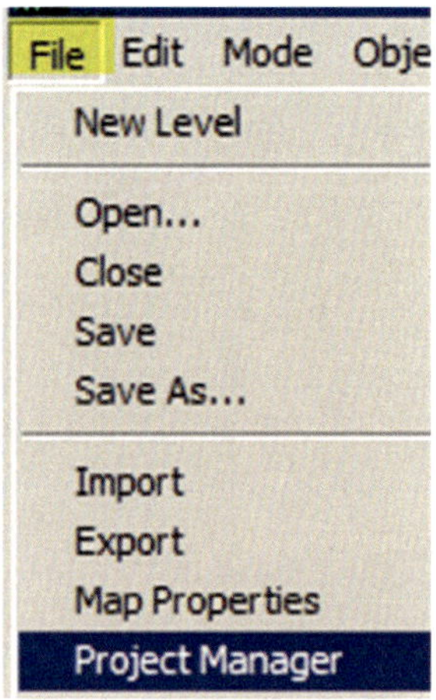

figure 6-11

The **Template Project** was selected and now we will see what scripts and actions are in that particular template script.

The **Project Manager** builds a game project from predefined, customizable Template Scripts.

Template Scripts can be combined and customized.

2 **Open the drop down menu for Class ➔ Click on SHOOTER (game genre)**

After aTemplate Project is selected in the Map Properties menu the Project Manager lists the **Classes** and the **Scripts** that are available for that particular template project.

Here you can ADD, REMOVE, CUSTOMIZE and UPDATE the game scripts.

Add a Template Script

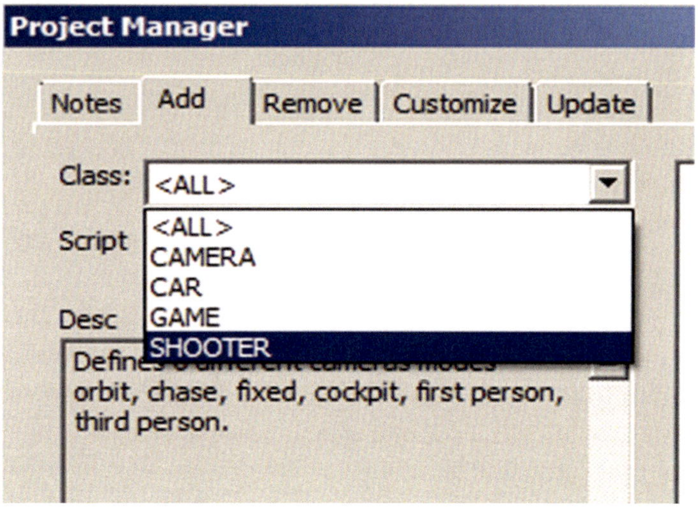

ADD
Adds a Template Script.

The example in this book is using the Shooter Template Script.

Each of the choices have different scripts and actions.

figure 6-12

Project Manager continued

Add a Template Script continued

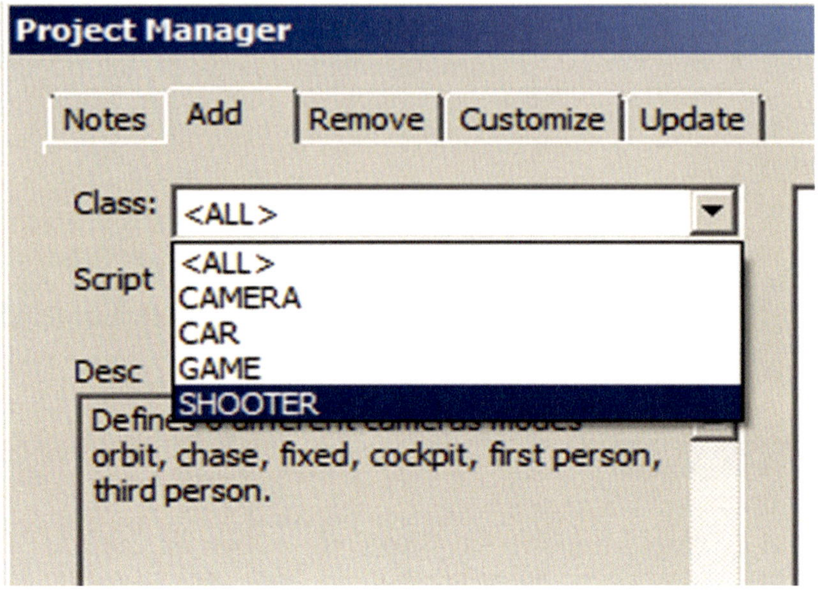

figure 6-13

Info.

ADD - Adds a Template Script. Templates are divided into different classes; camera, car, game, shooter. Each of these classes contain more scripts. And each of these scripts contain actions that can be attached to entities.
When you add a Template Script it is automatically copied from the templates/code folder to the work folder and the script is automatically included in the main game script.

REMOVE - Removes the template script. (only if the functions in that script are no longer needed for your project.)

CUSTOMIZE - **First highlight the script you want to customize - then click on Customize - the Customize Script panel opens for the Player Parameters script.** figure 6-13
The customize tab only modifies the Local Template Script copy that was created in the work folder.

UPDATE - This updates the script from a newer set of templates. By using Update you don't lose the customized parameters. This would be used after you download an upate of the Gamestudio software.

After selecting the CLASS Shooter the scripts under that class will be available to add to your game.

3 **Continue to ADD Scripts: ➔ CLICK on ADD SCRIPT ➔ the scripts load in the Project Manager. Continue to add scripts till the three scripts shown in figure 6-15 are added; Customizable Enemies, Player Parameters and Weapons and Power-ups.**

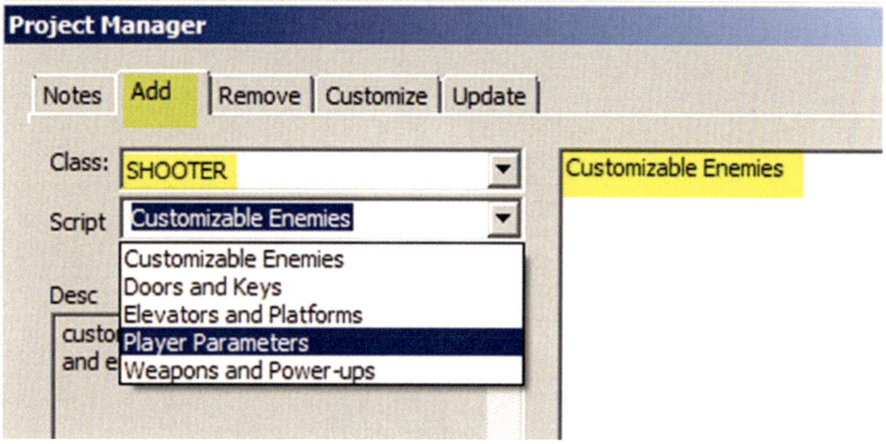

figure 6-14

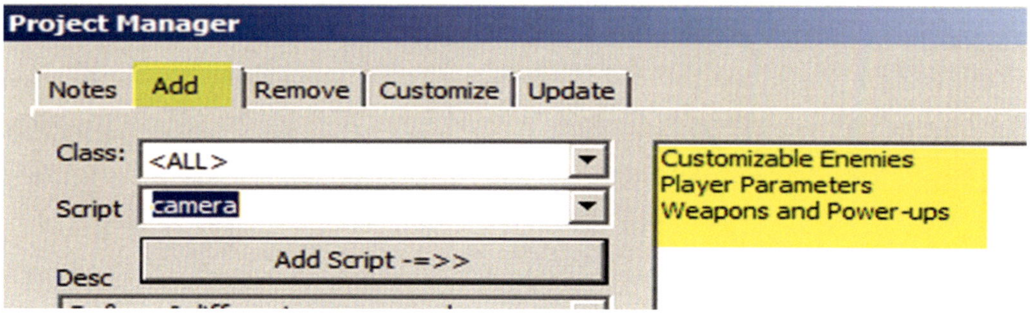

figure 6-15

The scripts and actions that have been added will be added to the entities in the WED level.

FOURTH - next step in creating a game - add players (entities)

Adding Players

1 **To bring a Model into the Gamestudio WED level Click Object ➔ Add Model ➔ Open the Work Folder - Open the LEVELS8 Folder - OPEN Actors Folder ➔ Choose an Actor to load into the level Click OK.** figure 6-16

2 **We are loading the Enemy model ➔ Enemy loads into the File Level (figure 6-17) ➔ Click on the Enemy name in the LEVELS TAB to highlight the model and make it "active". Use the MOVE Tool** 

If the Enemy has loaded into the level up in the air, PULL the Enemy down and place it just above the floor. figure 6-18 Remember to place the models that need to move around in the game just slightly above the floor. If they are placed on the floor line they may get stuck and not be able to move.

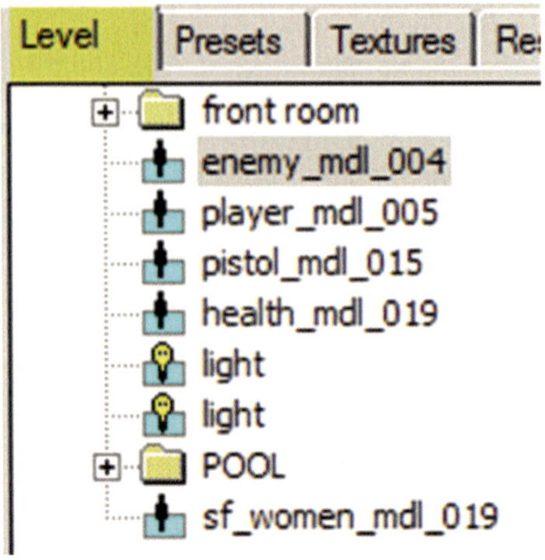

figure 6-17

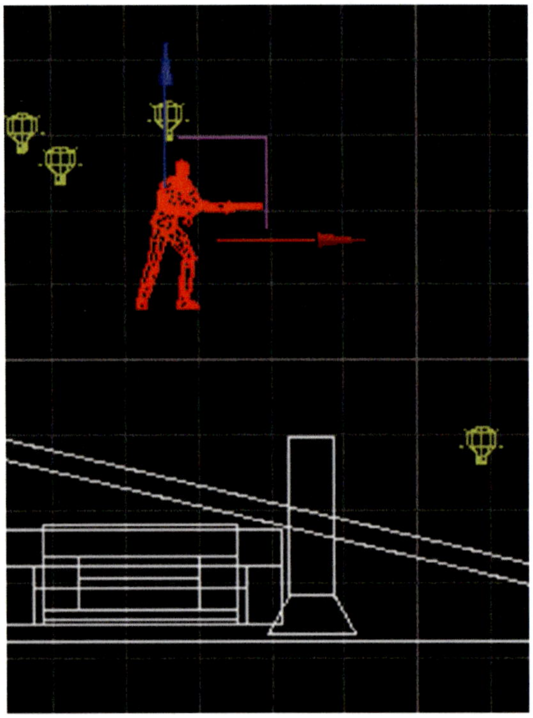

figure 6-18
Enemy Player above floor. Pull the player down to just above the floor.

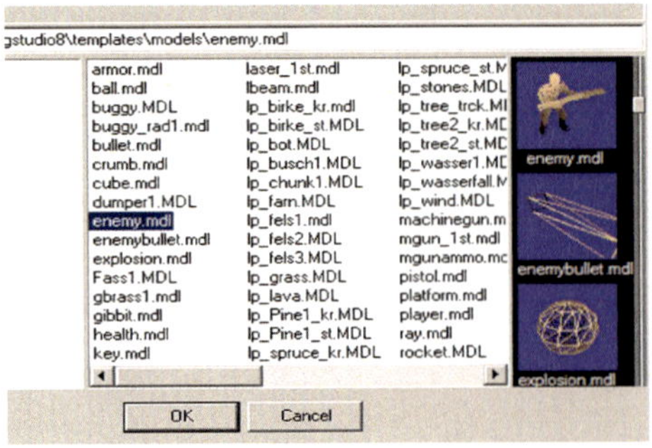

figure 6-16

Enemy_mdl figure 6-19

sf_women_mdl figure 6-20

4 You should see the actor you added inside the level, after pulling the actor down to just above the floor. **POSITION AND ROTATE THE MODEL** in preparation for game action. Activate the Rotate Tool. The Rotate arrows perform different functions in the different view windows in the WED level. XY Top View, YZ Side View, XZ Back View.

5 **Add other models to the level.** Follow the steps 1 thru 4. The book's example has added the Enemy model. This example will also be adding "player_mdl, pistol_mdl, health_mdl and sf_women_mdl. The number at the end of the names changes.
Be sure to **position the players around the level and rotate them for the start of a game.** This level will have one "player" and the camera view will be through his point of view. Two enemies are in the level. When the player walks close enough to the enemies the enemies will react and shoot at the player.

Place the models far enough away from each other so they don't start interacting with each other as soon as the game starts. You want to have the players walk toward each other before action begins at the start of the game.

FIFTH - next step in creating a game - Actions, Behaviors, Customizing

Actions, Behaviors & Customizing Players

With each script that is added various "actions" are listed in the WED level. When the player entity is highlighted - (this could the gun or the player or a car) - the "Actions" folder in the Behavior Tab will contain actions that can be assigned. This is a general folder of actions for the Shooter Game. Not all the actions can be interchanged between the entities. Generally t_shooter_enemy will go with a player who is an enemy and t_shooter_player is assigned to the main character. The "Health Pac" will be used in this game and its action is t_shooter_health. When the player runs up to the health pac a sound will activate and the health pac will disappear and the player gets more health points. Our two enemies will interact with the main character - player - and with some practice a person playing the game should be able to shot one of the enemies and run up to the health pac and continue fighting against the other enemy.

After all the entities have been added and their behaviors assigned then you can open File - Project Manager and customize the players and their actions.

figure 6-21

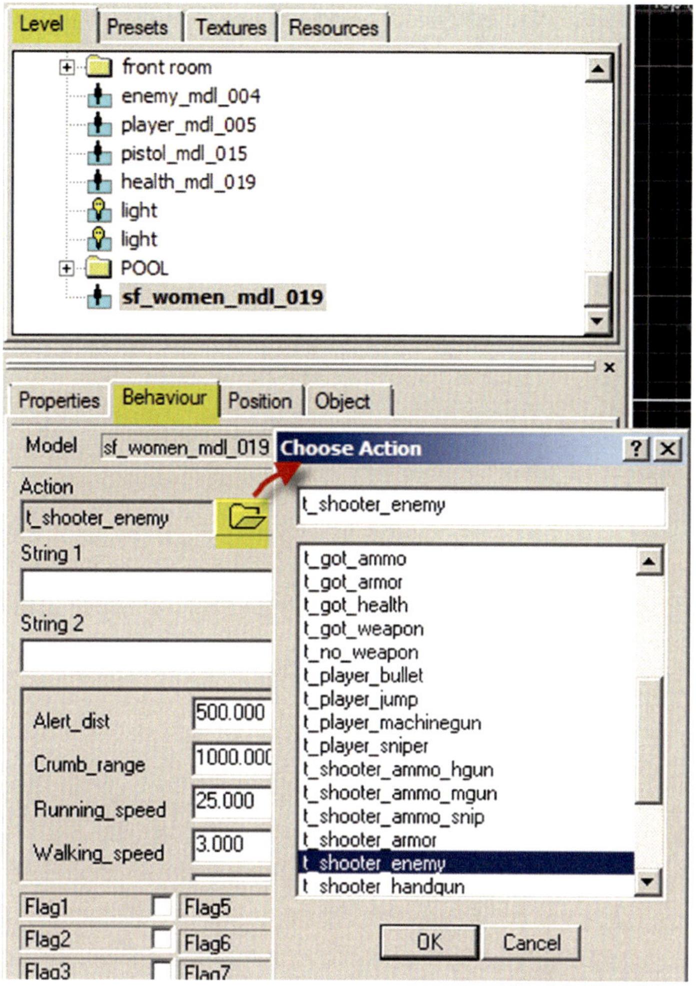

figure 6-22

1 **Highlight sf_women_mdl ➔ Click on the Level Tab ➔ Click on Behaviors Tab ➔ CLICK on ACTION FOLDER ➔ Select t_shooter_enemy ➔ Click on OK and File ➔ Save.**

2 **Repeat this for each model you load into the level. Cars and weapons get actions. These actions are generated from the Template Script that was checked earlier.**

Actions, Behaviors & Customizing Players

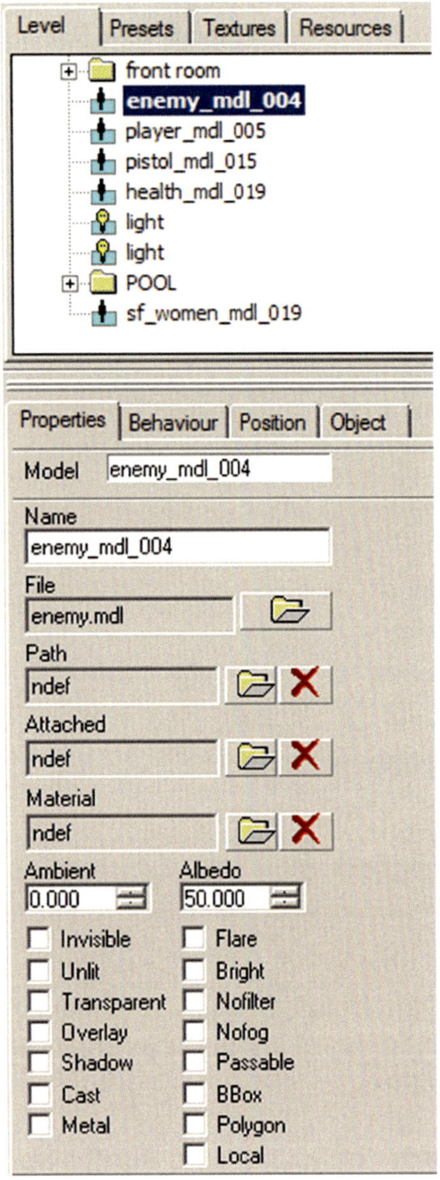

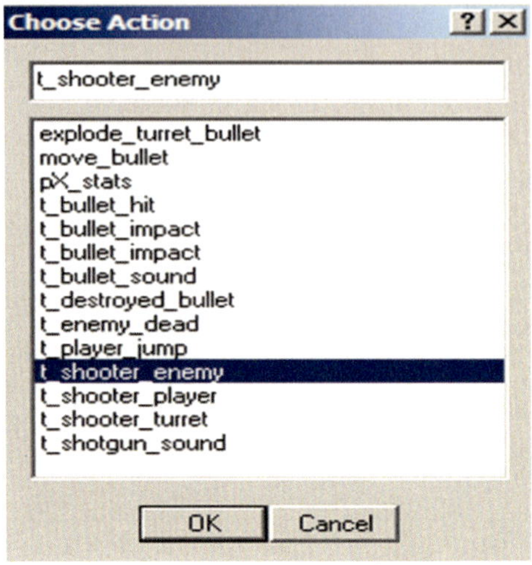

figure 6-24

The second enemy added to the game also has the t_shooter_ enemy action assigned to it.

Properties Tab for enemy_mdl

figure 6-23

3 Highlight enemy_mdl ➔ Click on the Level Tab ➔ Click on Behaviors Tab➔ Click on Action Folder➔ Select t_shooter_enemy ➔ Click on OK and File ➔ Save.

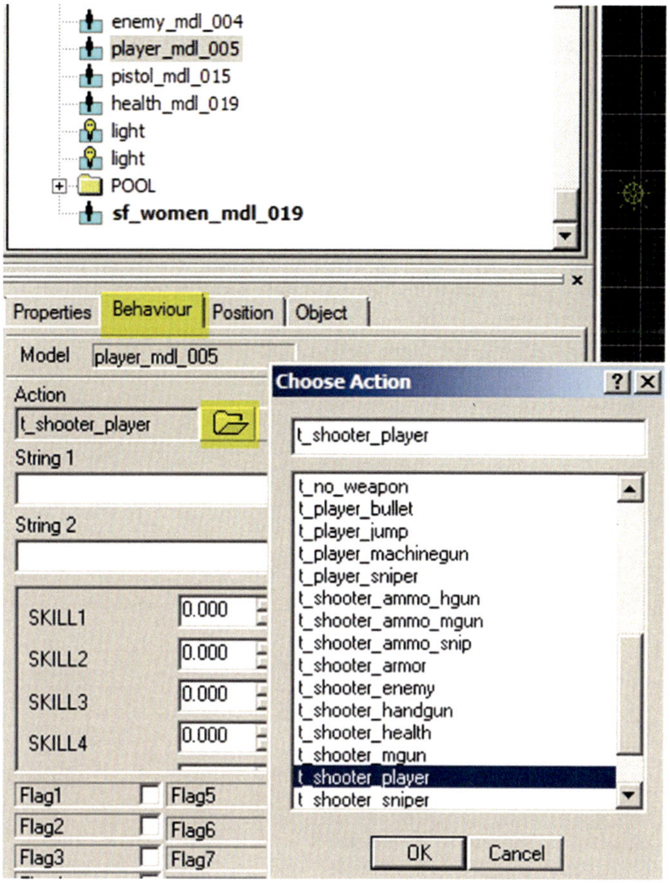

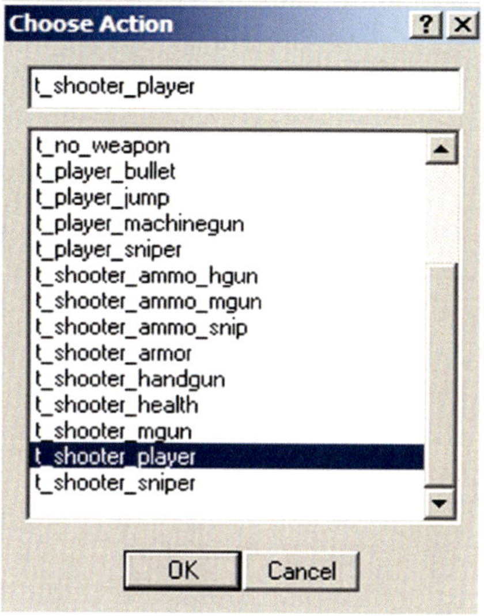

Action assigned: figure 6-26
t_shooter_player

player_mdl figure 6-25

4 Highlight player_mdl ➔ Click on the Level Tab ➔ Click on Behaviors Tab ➔ Click on Action Folder ➔ Select t_shooter_player ➔ Click on OK and File ➔ Save.

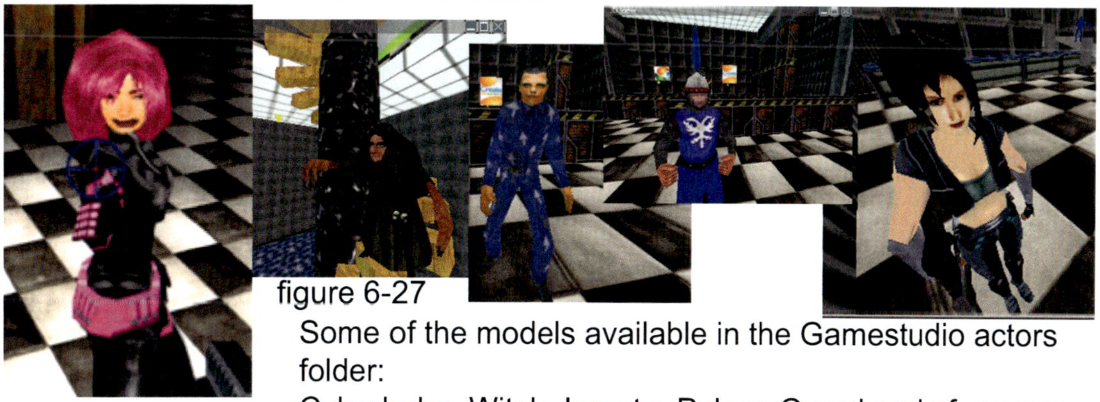

figure 6-27
Some of the models available in the Gamestudio actors folder:
Cyberbabe, Witch, Inmate, Palace Guard and sf_women.

Actions, Behaviors & Customizing Players

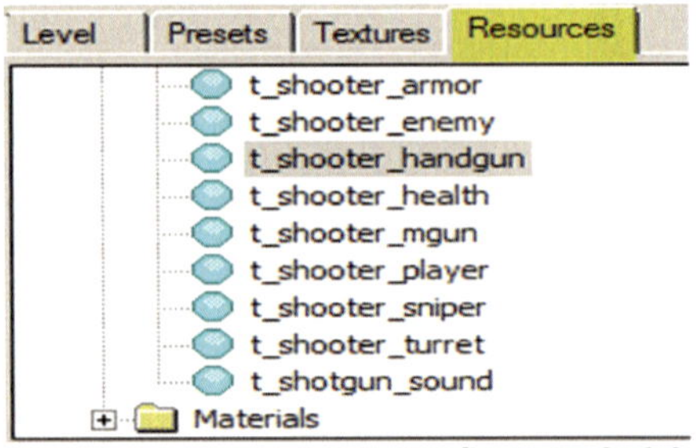

figure 6-28

Our example is assigning the t_shooter_handgun "action" to the pistol.
Other gun actions can be assigned to this gun. Some of the other gun actions show a burst of fire with each shot.

5 Highlight pistol_mdl ➔ Click on the Level Tab➔ Click on Behaviors Tab ➔ Click on Action Folder ➔ Select t_shooter_handgun ➔ Click on OK and File ➔ Save.

6 Highlight health_mdl ➔ Click on the Level Tab ➔ Click on Behaviors Tab ➔ Click on Action Folder ➔ Select t_shooter_health ➔ Click on OK and File ➔ Save.

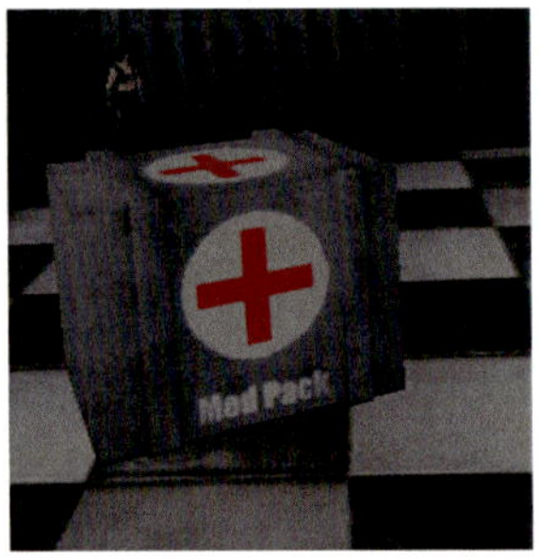
figure 6-29

This health pac will spin if placed just above the floor.

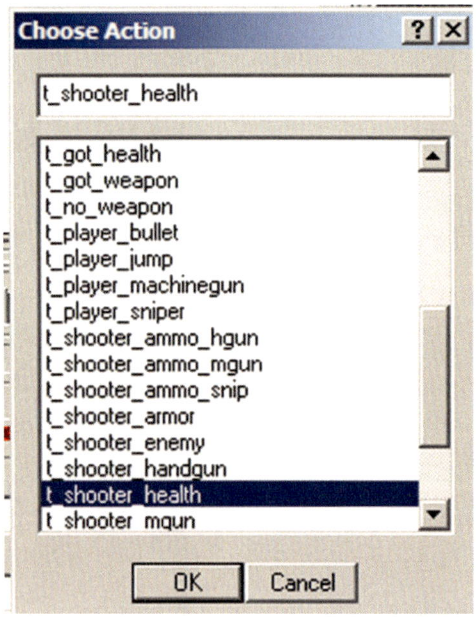

figure 6-31

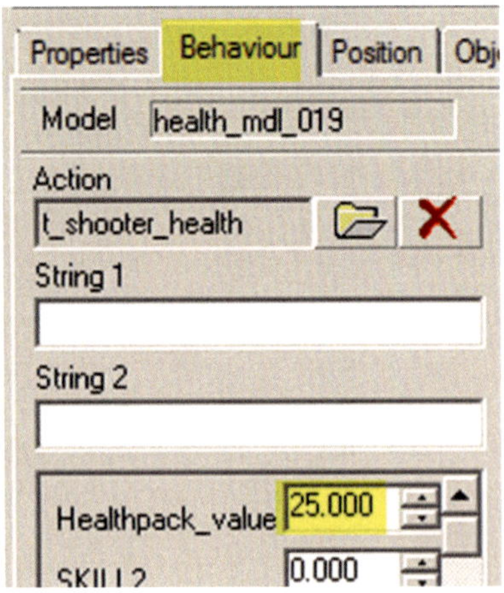

figure 6-30

The health points and the armor for a player can be set on the Behavior tab.

Be sure to assign an action to the entities you place inside the level, unless the entity is a tree or piece of furniture or something that is static and does not require action.

Customizing the Weapons, Players and Enemies

1 In the WED, Click on File ➔ Project Manager ➔ Customize Tab

2 Click on Player Parameters ➔ with player parameters highlighted Click on Customize Buttons ➔ the Customize Script pop up window appears.

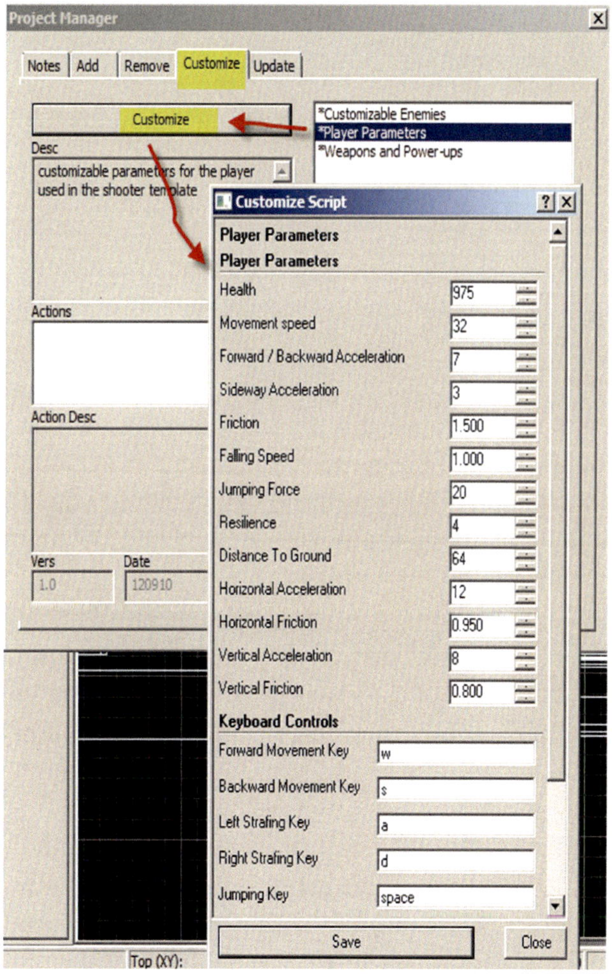

figure 6-32

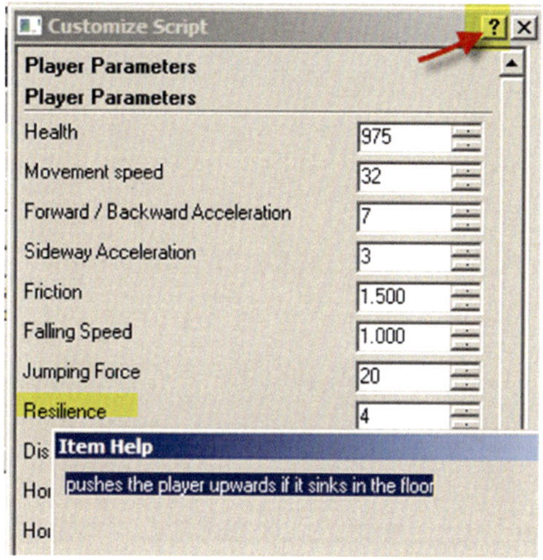

figure 6-33

Most of the actions are self explanatory. If you have a question about any of the actions Click on the **?** at the top of the window and then Right Click on an action (example: Resilience) to see the definition.

Customizing the Weapons, Players and Enemies

Examples of matching entities and actions:
armor_mdl = t_shooter armor
machinegun_mdl = t_shooter_mgun
snipergun_mdl = t_shooter_sniper
turret_mdl = t_shooter_ammo_hgun
mgunammo_mdl = t_shooter_ammo_mgun
sniperammo_mdl = t_shooter_ammo_sniper

The three action scripts that set player's ammo individually- t_shooter_ammo_hgun, t_shooter_ammo_mgun and t_shooter_ammo_sniper

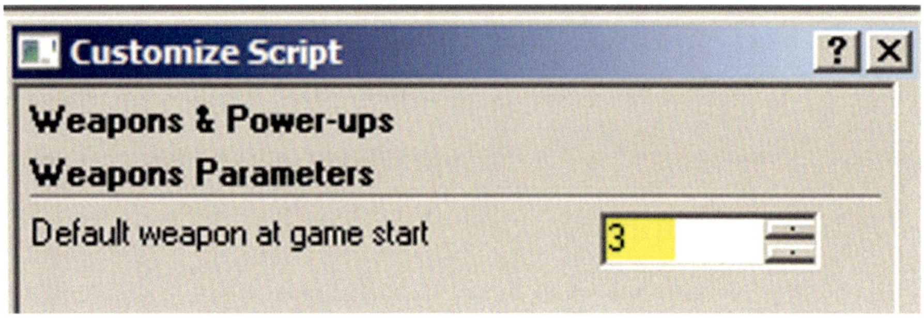

figure 6-34

Project Manager ➔ Customize Tab 0 = no weapon

SKIP to page 98 if you want to continue with the game creation.
This section explains additional information not used in this chapters example.

THE SHOOTER GAME - other elements

The shooter game code adds: t_shooter_player, t_shooter_weapons, t_shooter_enemies, t_shooter_elevators and t_shooter_doors.

The t_shooter_weapons.h file: adds the handgun, machine gun, sniper shooter, amo packs, ammo for machine gun, ammo for sniper, health packs and armor and armor ammo. Not all the these elements need to be used. The book's example is not using many of these elements. Only one weapon has been added to our game.

The t_shooter_enemies.h file: has script that adds two enemies, a turret that fires either rockets or bullets and a biped enemy (t_shooter_enemy). The Smooth Breadcrumb Path refers to the smoothness of the path that is followed by the enemies during a chase. Don't set the number for Breadcrumb to high or the enemy won't be able to follow the the player's tracks.

Customizing the turrets parameters:
Rockets - set the firing ammo of the turret. 0 = bullets, 1 = rockets
Turret_armor - initial turret armor.
Turret_angle - horizontal scanning angle, set a small value so the "player" can sneak around in the game and not be detected unless the player walks in front of the turret.
Turret_range - player detection range
Rocket_vertex - starting point for the rockets.
Mgun_vertex1 thru 6 - starting points for the bullets.
Bullet_damage - shows damage by the turret during the firing.
Rocket_damage - damage by the turret if it is firing rockets.

Enemies
Alert dist - if the player walks into this alert distance the enemy can see him and attack
Crumb_range - enemy's sensitivity to the player's invisible footprints. The default value is set at 1000 quants and if the player's footprints come within that distance the enemy chases the player guided by the player's invisible footprints.
Walking_speed - enemy walking speed during patroling
Running_speed - enemy running speed during chase
Dist_to_ground - sets enemy distance to the ground and his feet
Health - health points
Bullets_freq - frequency of bullets, set a small value and bullets fire more often
Shotgun_damage - amount of health points lost by the "player" every time the enemy hits the player

Elevators and Doors
Elevator_height - in quants sets when to stop
Elevator_speed - vertical speed
Elevator_wait - default is set at 4 seconds
Platform_offset - horizontal distance of the platform
Platform speed - movement speed
Platform_wait - can be set for X axis and Y axis depending on type of platform

Customizing the Weapons, Players and Enemies

SHOOTER GAME- continued

Doors and Keys
Unlimited number of doors can be set using keys or not using keys. They can operate on the X, Y or Z axis. Be creative use gates, bridges, barriers. Hide the key in a block and make the block invisible yet passable and the player can discover the key.
Attach t_shooter_door action to the door model
Key - indicates which key opens which door. Key = 0 (no key required)
Offset_x, Offset_z, Offset_y determines the direction the door moves.
t_shooter_key action has to be attached to the key model
Key set at 1 will open all doors set to Key 1
Key set at 2 opens doors set to Key 2 - continue with an unlimited amount of keys and doors matching.

SIXTH - next step in creating a game - save, build, run

1 **File ➔ Save As ➔ Click Save**

2 **Click on Build**

3 **Map Compiler Window opens ➔ Click OK**

4 **Click on Run ➔ the Run Level Window appears ➔ Click OK**

A Separate Game Window appears.

Press "F5" several times to increase the size of the game window and display the game full screen.

PLAYING THE GAME
Use the "W" key to move your character forward.

Use the "S" key to move your character backward.

The "A" key moves left.

The "D" key moves right.

Navigate around the room.

PLAYING THE GAME

Walk the player along and sneak up on the enemies. If you fire first you may be close enough to activate the other players to fire. However, you need to be within a certain distance. Try to capture the rotating health pac.

CLICK the LEFT MOUSE BUTTON to fire the weapon.

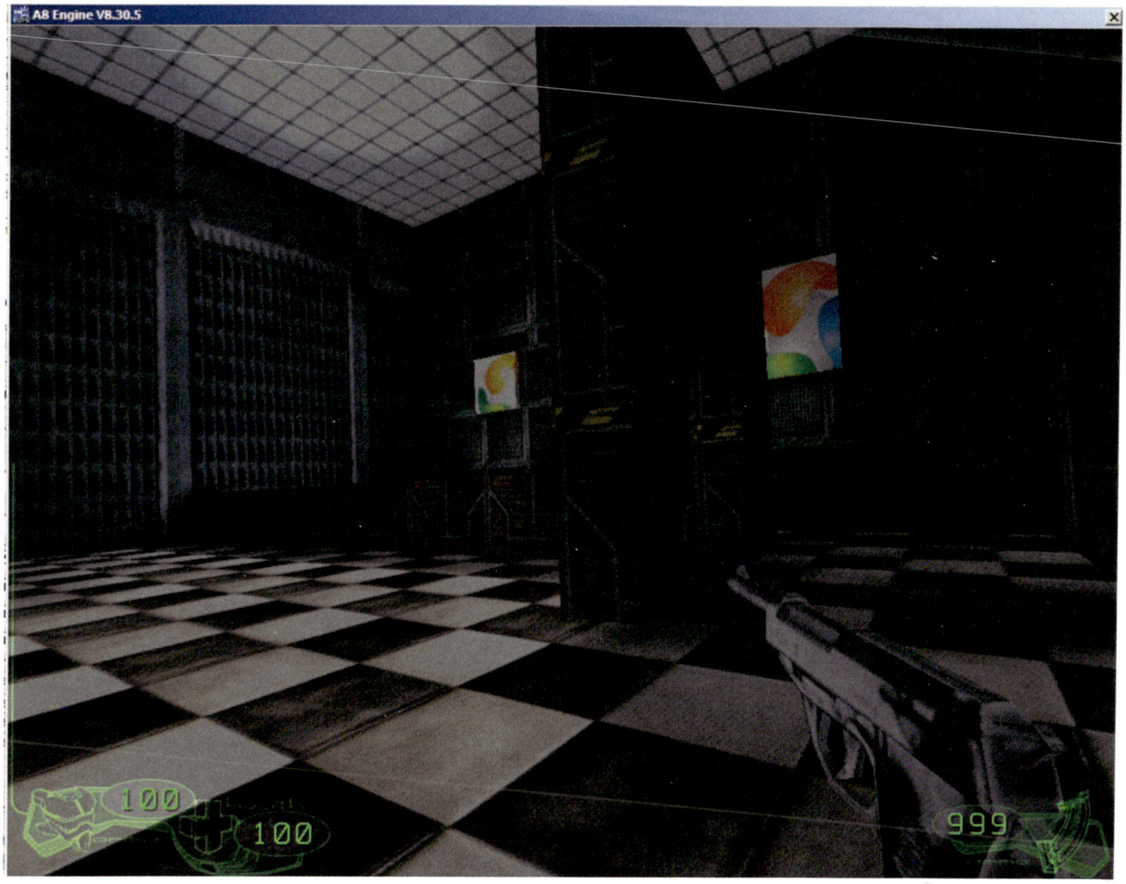

figure 6-35

Turn the volume up on your computer so you can hear the game. If a pool of water was added you should hear the water as you walk closer to the water.

PLAYING THE GAME

figure 6-36

figure 6-37

figure 6-38

figure 6-39

Enemy will turn and fire on the player

Second enemy figure 6-40

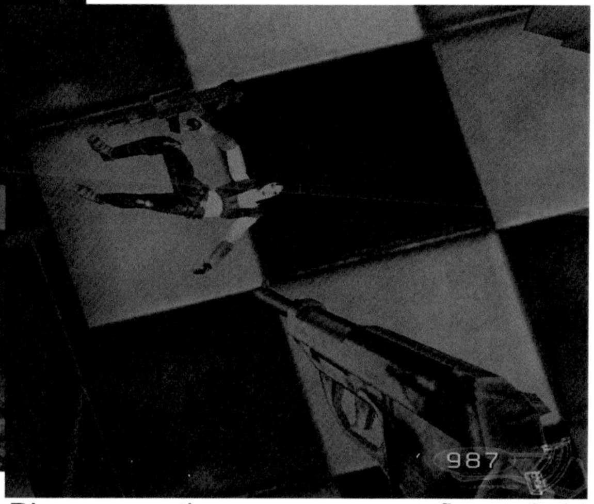

Player won the game. figure 6-41

Planning and Creating a Game

Will this game be for personal use or marketed and sold? Creating a commercial game requires level design, script programming, modeling, and shader programming. There are many examples of people who have successfully marketed their games. Gamestudio software has been used to design a variety of games. The most sophisticated game created to date with the software has been "3D Driving Academy." The game with the most distributable copies is , "Great Clips Racing". To find other examples and read the game licensing agreement visit.
http://www.conitec.com.

"NO ROYALTIES "
"As owner of any Gamestudio single edition you can freely publish and distribute your applications. You don't need to pay royalties, you don't need to show credits, you don't need to ask for permission. There is only one exception. It's illegal to use Gamestudio for games that propagate genocide against a certain group, race, nation or religion existing in today's real world."
For the license see www.3dgamestudio.com/license_eng.htm
FROM Conitec Gamestudio website 2012

Chapter 7 - **Publishing a Game**

Games created with Gamestudio can run on Windows Computers. To publish your game **CLICK on FILE ➔ PUBLISH** (have Compile EXE checked).

Do not use any spaces or different keyboard characters (dashes symbols etc.) in the game name.

The published game will be created in its own folder within the Gamestudio WORK Directory. All of the files within this folder are needed to run and distribute the game.

figure 8-1

Conitec Gamestudio Manual online

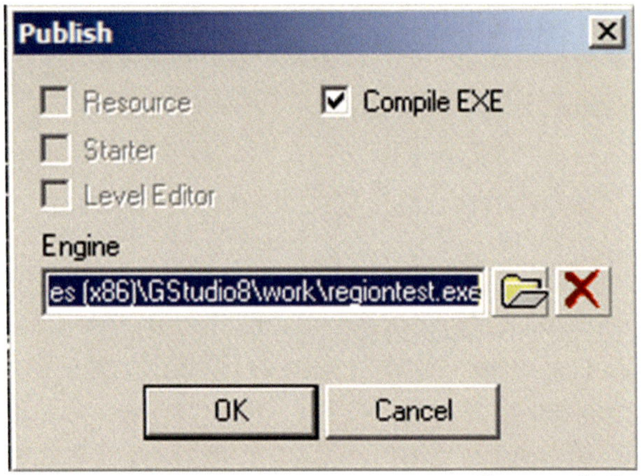

Check EXE figure 8-2

"The publish process creates a .CD subfolder in the work directory, and copies all files needed for the project into it. The content of the .CD folder can then be put onto CD-ROM or on a website for distribution. In the free version, most options are greyed out - just click [Ok] for starting the publish process."

"Please note: For creating the .CD subfolder, the work folder must be write enabled under Windows Vista or above! Therefore don't create your projects in the Gamestudio installation folder (which is normally only write enabled for the administrator under Vista), but in the Documents section of your PC."

Conitec Website Manual 2012

Complete information about publishing your game can be found at this location: http://www.conitec.net/beta/acknex.htm

Appendix A

CREATING A PATH FOR A PLAYER

1 **First add a second enemy. Then attach the t_shooter_enemy action to that player. This player can be a guard who walks a set path.**

2 **Click on OBJECT add PATH**

3 **Click on VERTEX NODES**

4 **ADD the first node.**

5 **Move your mouse along a path stopping to click and adding additional nodes. The nodes will appear with red lines attaching each node to the other. After completing the path go back and right click on each node, and give individual skill levels to the nodes in the path.**

6 **Next click on the player you want to walk along that path and highlight them red.**

7 **Under the Properties Tab attach the path you created (it will have a path number) to the player.**
When the game starts that player will automatically walk that path. If an additional an enemy is in the game, when you start firing your gun at the first enemy, both enemies will be firing at you.

PATH FOR PLAYER
Yellow line shows path with nodes set along the path.
Models who act as guards have paths set. Create a circle or oval path.

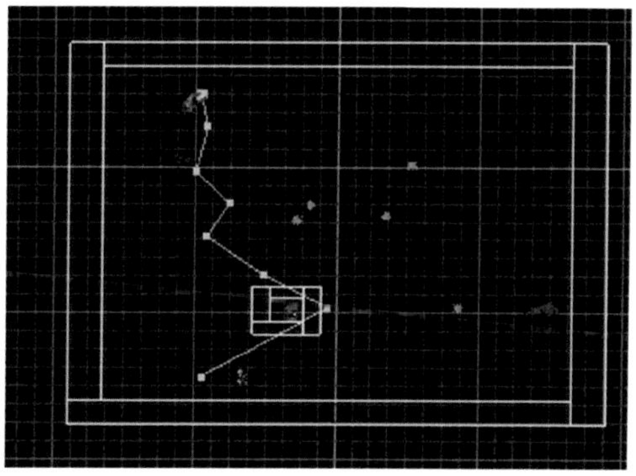

figure 1

Appendix B

SKY CUBE & OUTDOOR LIGHTING

Sky Cubes encompass the entire game level. They are textured with sky textures. The game level should just float above the bottom of the sky cube.

Sky textures and water textures can be animated. This example is using the non-animated sky texture in the main Gamestudio standard wad texture pack.

figure 1-1

standard.wad contains a sky cube texture of an outdoor scene. When you apply the texture to your sky cube it appears tiled. figure 1-2

figure 1-2

The Sky Texture has a tiled pattern and needs to be fixed. Check Sky Cube under the Preferences Tab.

1 **Create a large hollowed cube that wil encompass the entire game level.**

2 **Highlight the new cube and texture it with a sky texture.**

3 **If the sky texture appears as a tiled pattern then Click on File - Preferences - and go to the Object Options and CHECK the Sky Cube Box.** figure 1-1, figure 1-2

After checking the Sky Cube Box the tiled pattern will appear as one unified scene.

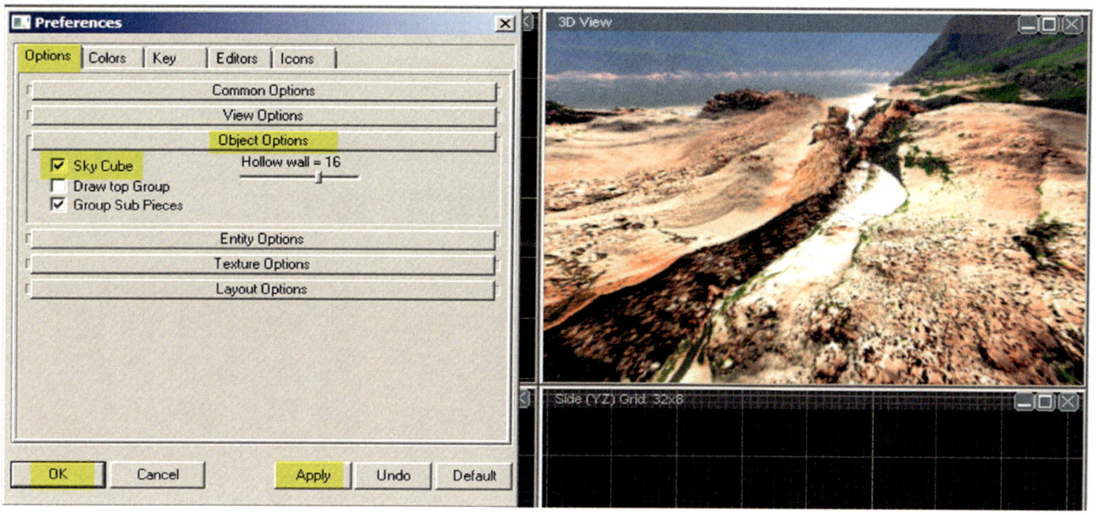

figure 1-3

4 **Next, the lighting for the Sky Cube can be set by Clicking on File - Map Properties and then Clicking SUN.**
The settings for the sun can be set. They are Sun Azimuth, Sun Elevation, Sun, and Ambient.

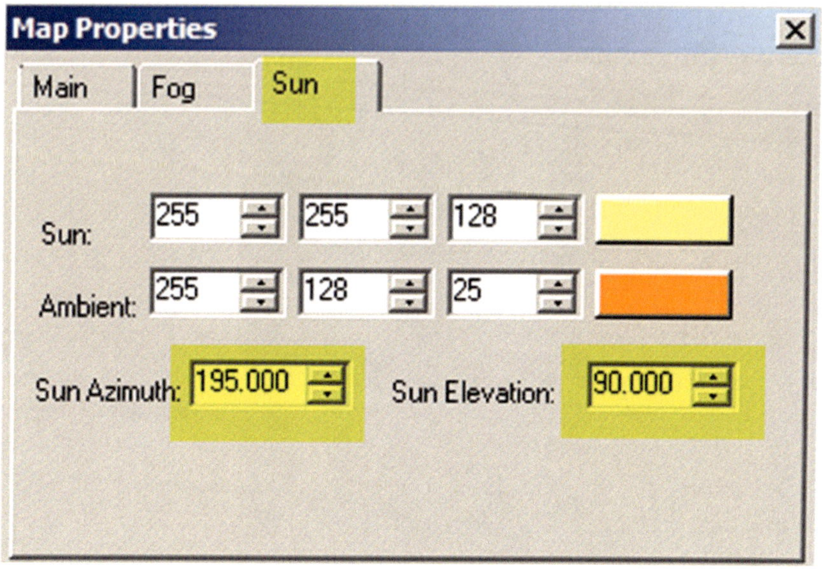

figure 1-4

Lighting is important. Light highlights certain areas and creates atmosphere. The outdoor scenes can be changed with the Sun setting and playing with the Azimuth and the Sun Elevation. In figure 1-4 the Sun is set at a pink color and the ambient light is white. The results are shown in figure 1-5 for this setting.

AMBIENCE = BRIGHTNESS

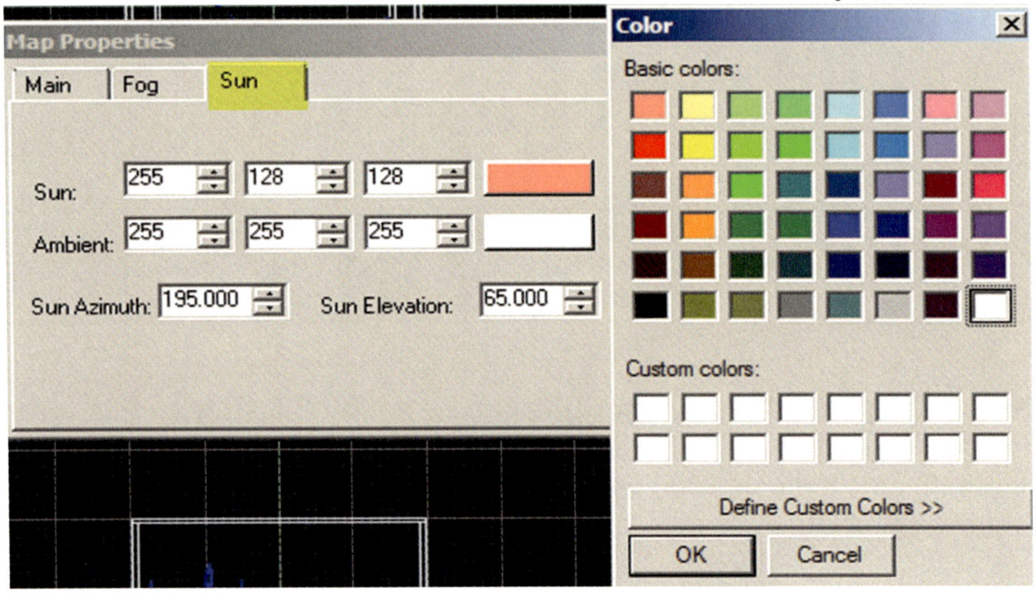

figure 1-5

To cast a shadow
- highlight an object and check Shadow and Cast on the Properties Tab.

figure 1-6

Ambient Light = Ambient Intensity * Ambient Color

Diffuse light is emitted by dynamic light sources and by the sun. Diffuse light reflects light equally in all directions.

figure 1-7

Examples of different light settings for the same outdoor scene.

figure 1-8

TERRAGEN is a free software program you can use to create sky cube textures from your own graphics. The free version cannot be used for commercial purposes. Terragen renders and animates realistic environments.
http://www.terragen.org/

Appendix C

SOUND

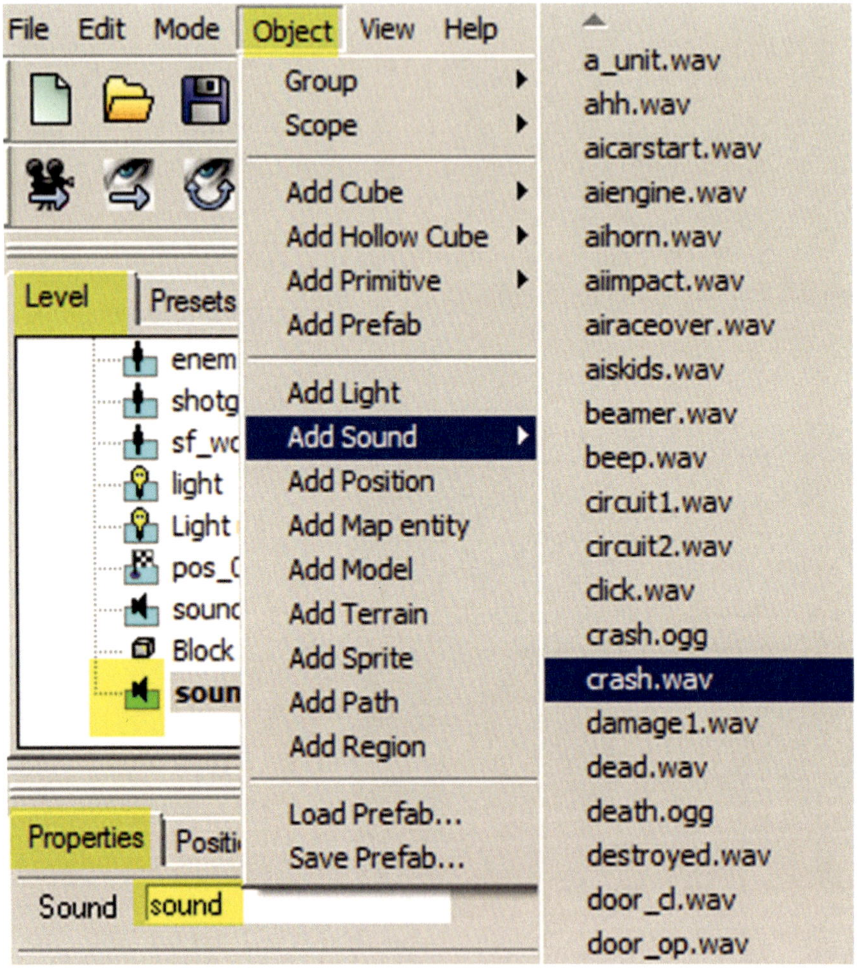

figure 1-1

The sound file .wav can be added to objects in the level. The sound usually increases in volume the closer a player gets to the object which has an attached sound. Highlight an object and click Object - Add Sound. There are key sounds for opening a door, and beepers that might indicate how close a player is walking to an invisible object. Sounds will add realism to the game.

Appendix D

Adding a Functioning Pool with Terrain and a Region

The earlier example in this book created pools that were for background scenery. Pools and areas in a level can have terrain added and the terrain can have an action script attached making the pool interact with players who swim through the water. Keep in mind compiling and rendering time for your game and give the important water elements action scripts and use other water elements as background scenery.

1 **Create a pool by creating a hollowed cube that is placed in the floor of an existing level.**

2 **Use CSG Subtract with an unhollowed cube to cut out the inside and top of the pool cube.**

3 **Click Object - Add Terrain** figure 1-1

4 **Select a Terrain from the Terrains folder inside the levels8 folder** figure 1-2, figure 1-3.

5 **Position the Terrain inside the empty hollowed pool. Resize the Terrain.**

6 **Highlight the Terrain and Click on the Behavior Tab and open the Action Folder and add an Action Script. figure 1-4** (This book is not covering scripting. The default templates in gamestudio do not have actions for terrain in the Shooter Template Script which was used in this book. Gamestudio has a lot of information online about scripting and using their Lite-C scripting program. Use the Empty Script Template and load your own script or download a script from the AUM magazine site, www.coniserver.net.)

7 **Highlight the Terrain and Click on the Properties Tab and CHECK Transparent and Passable.** figure 1-5

8 Click Object - Add Region - Resize the Region to encompass the pool area or an area in the level that has a terrain added. figure 1-6, figure 1-7

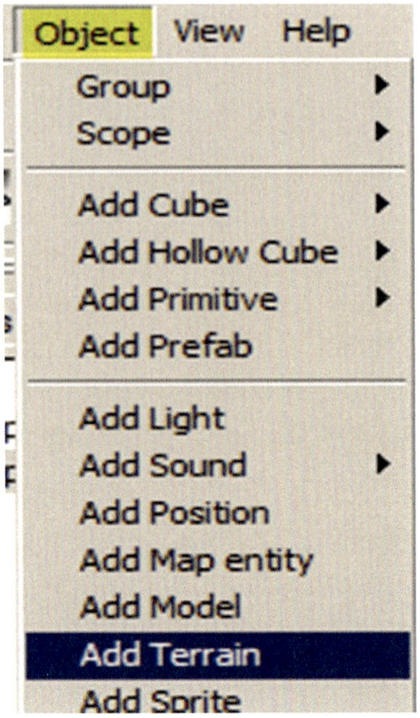

figure 1-1

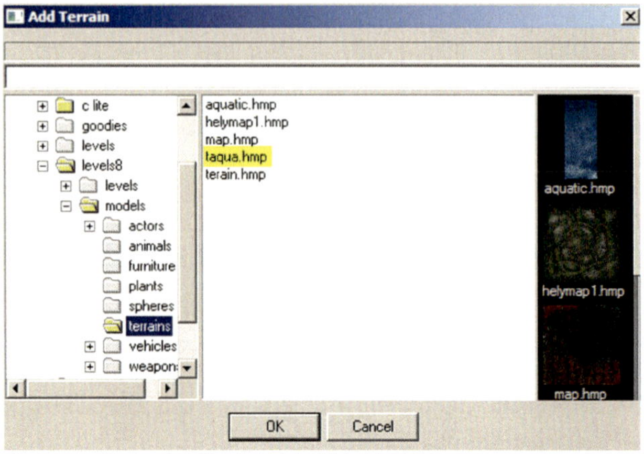

figure 1-3

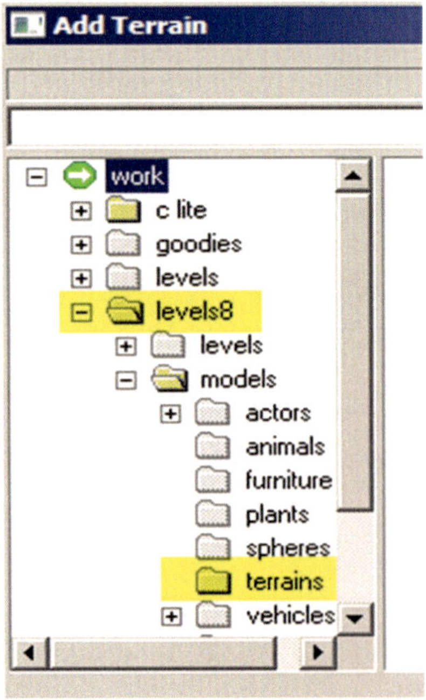

figure 1-2

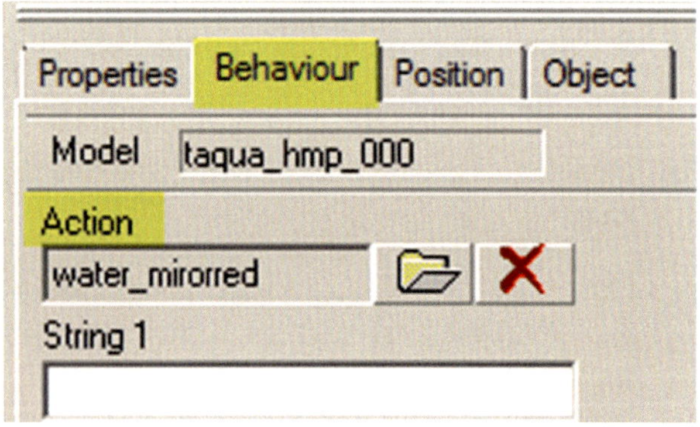

figure 1-4

9 With the terrain highlighted click on Behavior and choose an action for the terrain.

Adding a Functioning Pool with Terrain and a Region - continued

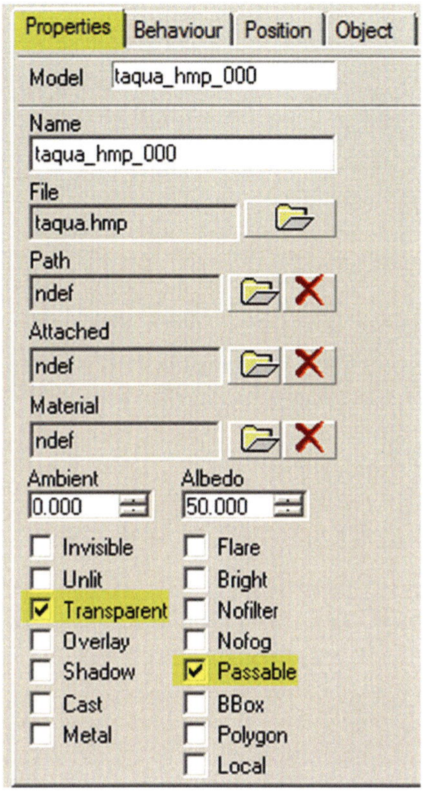

figure 1-5

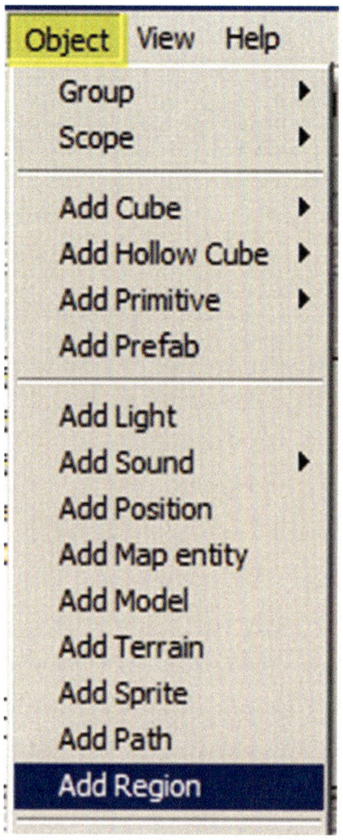

figure 1-6

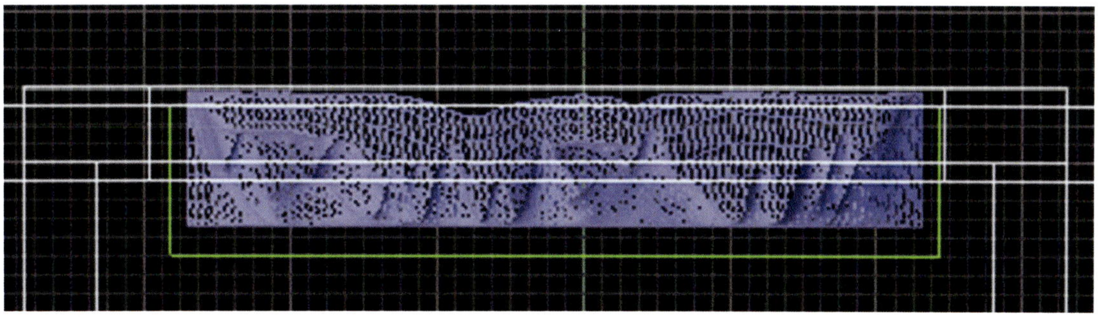

figure 1-7

In Version 8 terrains need a Region added, figure 1-7 shows the finished pool with the blue terrain added, the green line represents the region.

Appendix E

SCRIPT EDITOR INFO - SED

Conitec only provides a few template scripts in their 3D Gamestudio software. The templates are a beginning point for users. First you learn to create a level in the WED and how to load one of the template scripts into your level. The biggest advantage to having the Gamestudio finished template script is that you can open the code in the SED Script Editor and see how the game was created.

Conitec's website has a series of tutorials for learning the Lite-C sripting software.

To create your own games you have to learn the Lite-C software. Lite-C is based on the C/C++ programming language. Gamestudio provides 25 workshops to help you learn the Lite-C language. The workshop files can be viewed online or downloaded from:

http://server.conitec.net/down/litec_samples.zip

If you want to learn more about their Lite-C program visit their tutorial website :

http://tutorial.3dgamestudio.net/

"The lite-C package contains a complete development environment with 3D model and terrain editor, code editor, compiler, debugger, an integrated 3D engine, a physics engine, many samples including DirectX and OpenGL programs, and a tutorial with 24 easy workshops." *Conitec January 2010*

Script written in the World Definition Language (WDL); is used for programming games in Conitec's 3D Gamestudio. These are program source codes.

WDL files (earlier versions)/ .c files are saved in a text format. They can be opened and edited with a text editor. The Conitec Gamestudio Script language is C-Lite. Gamestudio's editor is the SED.

The SED Editor is where owners of Gamestudio create their own games using the Lite-C programming language. Version 8 now uses .c files. They replace the .wdl files.

The editors in the Gamestudio software are:
SED is the Lite-C Editor which is where the script coding is created, edited, compiled and debugged.
MED is the model and terrain editor where you can create and import 3D objects.
WED is the level editor.
GED- game editor
The major portion of this book has focused on the WED - the level editor.

Types of files:
.wdl WDL Script
.mdl Model
.hmp Terrain
.wmp WMP Level
.c Lite-C Script
.h Lite-C Header

Scripts have to end in ".c"
Scripts usually contain a function main
Functions contain numerous commands

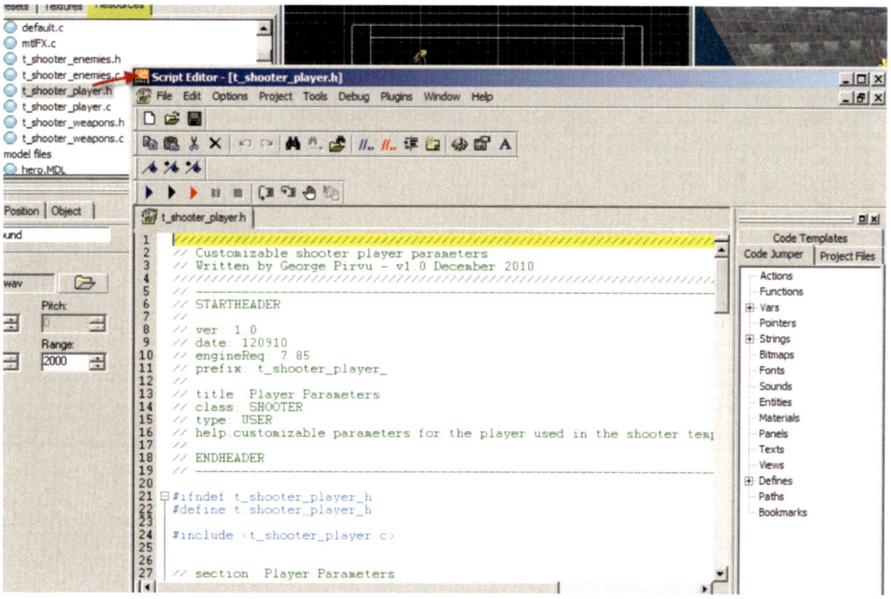

Where's the Code? Under the Resources Tab.

figure 1

Click on the Resources Tab, Open the Script folder and right click on t_shooter_player.h, click open and the SED editor opens with the header code for the t_shooter_player.

CODE - Action scripts start to run automatically when an entity is loaded. The actions are in the WED action list. Actions are used to control entities and they are functions that are attached to entities. They control the entities behavior. Action code can be viewed under the Actions folder in the Resources Tab.

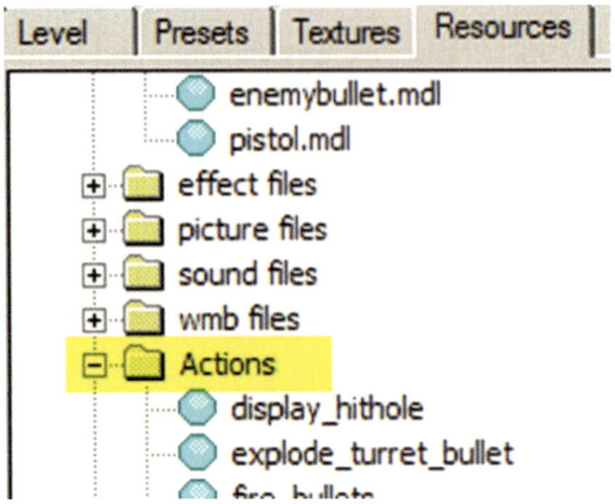

figure 2

Open the Resources Tab, Click on the Actions folder and click View Source to see the code assigned to an entity.

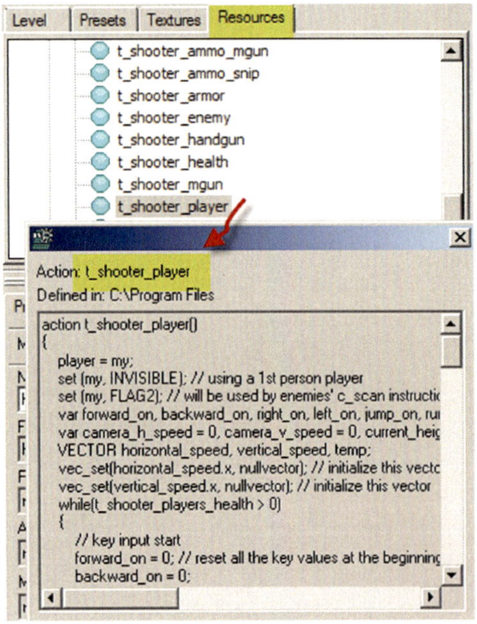

figure 3

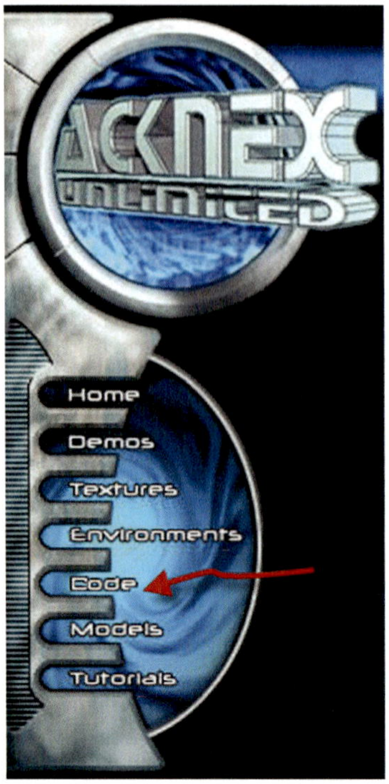

figure 4

Code available from Conitec.

Conitec provides code at their "Gamestudio Resource Site" but you must give the authors credit. http://au.conitec.net/

"There are three standard license policies:
Free - free for all GameStudio projects, without restrictions.
Credits - free for all GameStudio projects as long as your name is credited.
Limited - free for non-commercial GameStudio projects as long as your name is credited. Your requirements for a commercial project - like royalties - are mentioned in the readme.txt."
Conitec 2012 ACKNEX UNLIMITED

Intense X - is a game plug-in for the 3D Game Studio Engine. Intense X allows game designers with little or no programming experience to create games.

Appendix F

ODDS & ENDS

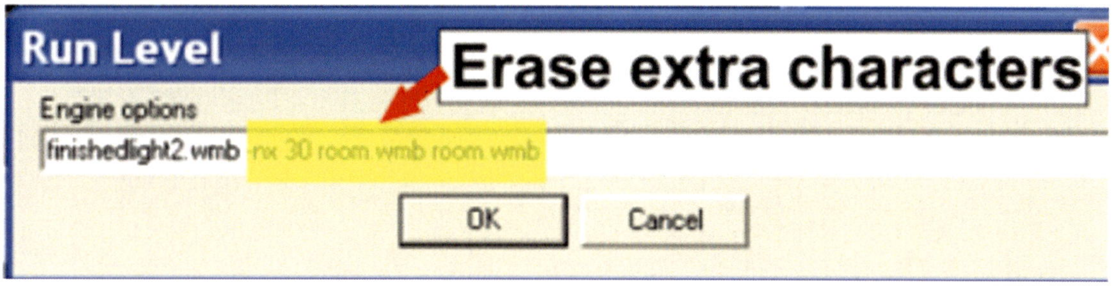

figure 1

PROBLEMS: Sometimes the **Run Level** adds extra characters at the end of the file extension and this prevents the file from running properly. To correct this, ERASE the Extra Characters after the .wmb before hitting OK on the Run Level. First try running the level and if the level won't run try this fix.(this was more common in earlier versions)

Pressing the insert key on the keyboard will show a popup menu of items that can be inserted like blocks, sound, terrain. It's a selection of items from the Object Menu.

[F2] Quicksave.
[F3] Quickload.
[F5] Video resolution up. (3 times)
[Shift-F5] Video resolution down.
[F6] Takes **screenshots** to the file "**shot_n.jpg**".
[F12] Toggles music and sound.
[Alt-F4] Shuts down the engine.
[Esc] Shuts down the engine.
[Alt-Enter] Toggles window and fullscreen mode.

Gamestudio Tools
http://www.coniserver.net/wiki/index.php/Free_Tools

PREFERENCES

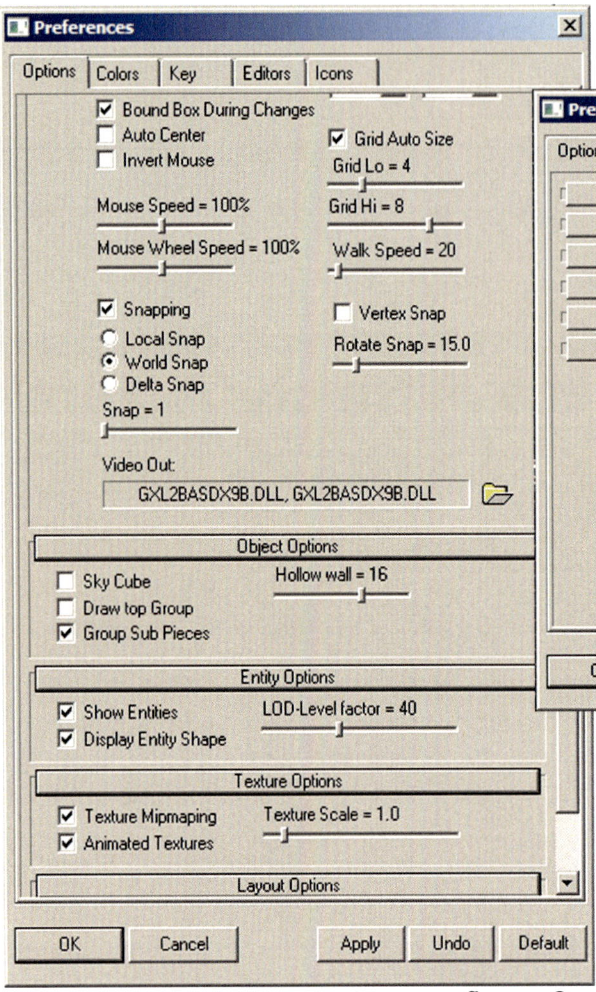

figure 2

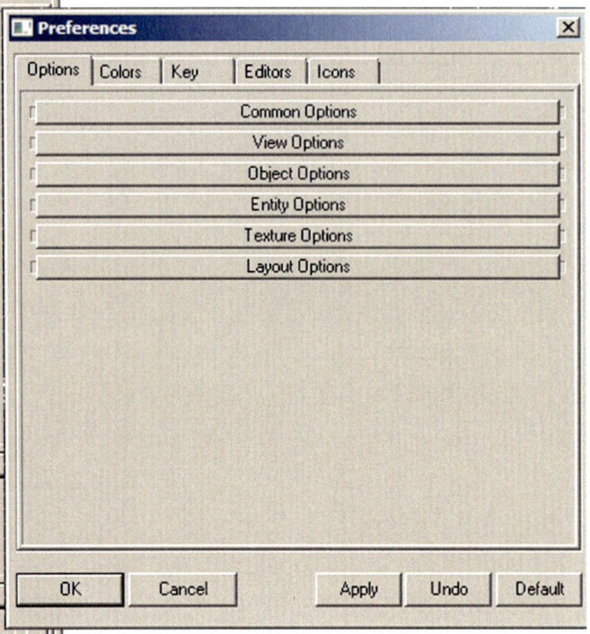

figure 3

CLICK ON FILE - PREFERENCES to open the Options, Colors, Key, Editors and Icons panels to make changes and set the preferences.

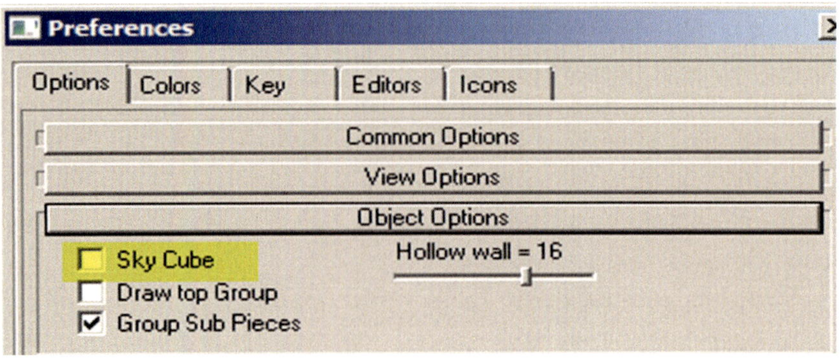

figure 4

WEBSITES AND OTHER LINKS OF INTEREST:

AUM (ACKNEX USERS MAGAZINE)
http://www.opserver.de/coni_users/web_users/pirvu/aum/aum1/english/aum1/index.html

http://aum.conitec.net/

Gamestudio Community Forum
http://www.opserver.de/ubb7/ubbthreads.php?ubb=cfrm

Gamestudio site's list of website links
http://www.conitec.net/english/gstudio/download.php

Mastery in Game Development
http://devmaster.net/

The Art and Business of Making Games
http://gamasutra.com/

http://www.educationarcade.org/

http://www.technologyreview.com/article/18678/
http://www.technologyreview.com/computing/?mod=Nav_Computing

International Game Developers Association
http://www.igda.org/

Digital Games Research Association
http://www.digra.org/

Game Research and Technoloy
http://www.red3d.com/cwr/games/

Create your own scenery
http://www.terragen.org/

Visual Index

New – Creates a new
level

Open – opens the file folder where the level is saved

Save – saves the present level to a file

Copy- copies the current selected object to the clipboard

Paste – creates a new instance of the saved object

Undo – reverts to the previous state

Redo

Build - Compiles the file

Run- Executes the file and opens a separate window showing the compiled file

Lock Selection – Locks the current selection unless menu functions are performed. (Select All, Select None etc)

Select None - Deselects all selections

Select

Move - Move the current selection

Rotate – Rotate selected object/objects up/down to rotate clockwise/ counterclockwise. Vertically dragging arrow rotates about the arrow axis. NOTE - do not rotate terrain.

Scale - current selection, hold down to scale proportionately

Edit Box – scales, rotates and moves the selected object. Pull on nodes to control object.

Slice Wire – Cut the selected object with a wire, press ENTER to cut.

Slice Plane – Cut the selected object with a plane, press ENTER to cut. The Slice Plane cuts an entire group along a plane.

Vertex Move – Move a vertex of the selected object. Applies to blocks or paths. Modify the shape of a block.

Edge Move - Move an edge on the selected object.

Face Move – Move a face on the selected object.

Mirror – Mirrors the current selection on the Axis.

Add Object – Add new object.

Delete Object - Deletes current selection.

8

Grid Scale

"Snap Mode - Toggle between **Local Snap L** (snap aligns on the object position), **Delta Snap D** (snap aligns on the move origin) and **World Snap W** (snap aligns on world coordinates)."
"Vertex Snap - Objects snap to the next vertex of another object within the same group."
"Snap Size - How many quants will an object be moved."
"Axis Restrict - Restrict movment to horizontal, vertial or both directions, or set the axis for the Mirror button."
Conitec Gamestudio Online Manual 2012

Camera Move If curser is on an object the object will spin around a center point.

Move Eye Changes the position of where the virtual "eye" is looking in the editing widows

Rotate Eye Changes the orientation of the view in the 3D edit window

Zoom Eye 3D view, increases and descreases distance between the 3D view's "eye" position and editing focus point.

Camera Position - Use to rotate the oject in 3D View. Set a point (green) and use the red point to move an object around the first set point. Place the look-at point in the 2D view, and drag to place the camera position.

Walk-Thru Use the mouse to look left, right, up and down. Move using the Arrow keys or the right mouse button. Pressing [Shift] doubles the speed. [Home] and [End] will move you vertically. [PgUp], [PgDn], and Left / Right let you turn about your main axes. Press [ESC], [SpaceBar], or the [Enter] key at any time to quit the Walk through Mode.

Scope Up / Scope Down - Scope Down "enter" the view, Scope Up "exits". When activated other objects disappear and only the scoped object is visible.

Scope Up - Scope one group level up.
Scope Down - Scope one group level down

INDEX

S

T

U

V

W

X

Y

Z

Made in United States
Orlando, FL
04 November 2026

90202577R00076